W9-ACE-836

1989

Probation and Parole

Rodney J. Henningsen

Sam Houston State University

Under the General Editorship of George G. Killinger,
Dean Emeritus, Sam Houston State University

HARCOURT BRACE JOVANOVICH, INC.

New York   San Diego   Chicago   San Francisco   Atlanta

London   Sydney   Toronto

These titles are currently available in the HBJ CRIMINAL JUSTICE SERIES:

Criminal Investigation   Jerry L. Dowling
Criminal Procedure and Evidence   Rolando del Carmen
Legal Aspects of Evidence   Robert W. Ferguson and Allan H. Stokke
Police Organization and Administration   Samuel S. Souryal
Probation and Parole   Rodney J. Henningsen

Books on the following topics are now in preparation:

Community Relations, Constitutional Law, Criminal Law, Criminology, Juvenile Delinquency, Law Enforcement, Police Report Writing

ISBN: 0-15-571980-7
Library of Congress Catalog Card Number: 80-85166
Printed in the United States of America

PREFACE

Throughout history, societies have responded in various ways to violations by their members of approved values, traditions, and rules. A typical response has been the banishment of the offender, a punishment effected in modern times by isolation in a prison or other penal institution. Today, however, the emphasis is on corrections, and our expectations go beyond the mere isolation of offenders from society. We assume that at the least offenders should be no worse for their correctional experience and at best they should be able to reintegrate themselves as productive and law-abiding members of society.

Significant tools in the furtherance of these expectations are the correctional practices of probation and parole. These community-based alternatives to traditional incarceration are the subject of this textbook for undergraduate students. The book examines probation and parole from several vantage points in order to bring their conceptual, historical, philosophical, structural, functional, and legal aspects into balanced focus. Discretionary decision making and the supervised release of offenders within the community are at the heart of probation and parole, and the text examines the role of professionals and volunteers in each of these critical areas.

Since the book is intended primarily as an introductory treatment for undergraduates, it has been written so as to facilitate comprehension and retention. It employs the outline format characteristic of the HBJ Criminal Justice series, with section titles in boldface type to make the issues and interrelationships clear to the reader. Technical terms are carefully explained, and numerous figures, tables, and examples have been included to illustrate the points raised. In short, the book provides a complete picture of probation, parole, and community corrections in a form that students can effectively absorb and master.

Rodney J. Henningsen

CONTENTS

I. RESPONSE OF SOCIETY TO CRIME AND CRIMINALS

Throughout the course of human experience, societies have responded to the violation of accepted values, traditions, and rules by their own members or by outsiders. This first chapter notes the types of responses made by different societies in various times, places, and cultures when their norms, or rules for behavior, have been violated. In most Western nations (including the United States), such responses have frequently been inspired by well-developed schools of thought concerning human nature and the best means for controlling undesired behavior; and these major schools are examined herein. Finally, the chapter discusses the current societal response to crime and criminals, with its emphasis on community-based corrections and the role of probation and parole in the corrections process.

A. TYPOLOGY OF SOCIETAL RESPONSES TO CRIME

The actions taken to deal with crime and criminals have varied widely over time and among societies. Nevertheless, it is possible to classify such actions under six basic types of response: banishment, retribution, expiation, deterrence, rehabilitation, and reintegration.

1. **Banishment**: Banishment is a traditional response to the violation of societal rules, and is essentially motivated by the desire to protect society from the violator (the criminal).

   a. **Primitive banishment**: Among primitive peoples, banishment from the group or tribe was the most common penalty meted out to criminals. Such peoples believed that the gods were angered by the offender, and that the whole tribe would be punished if the criminal were not banished. Banishment from the tribe usually meant death, since the offender seldom could survive on his own and was unlikely to be accepted by other tribes.

   b. **Modern forms of banishment**: In more recent times, commitment of offenders to isolated or fortress-type prisons (such as Alcatraz or Devil's Island) has served as a form of banishment. As in the case of primitive banishment, the goal is protection of society. But whereas primitive banishment sought to accomplish this by appeasing the gods, modern "banishment" seeks to protect society by reducing the contagion of crime (on the theory that offenders confined in prison cannot harm society).

2. **Retribution**: Retribution is one of the oldest and most common societal reactions to crime and criminals. "An eye for an eye and a tooth for a tooth" is the guiding principle for this response, whereby a wrong is corrected by treating the offender in similar fashion. Punishments ranging from death (in the form of beheading, boiling in oil, and the like) to humiliation or imprisonment have been imposed over the course of time as a means of achieving retribution.

   a. **Early procedures for retribution**: In primitive societies, the criminal's misdeeds were considered offenses against the victim or his family which could be met by a response in kind from the latter. This was especially true if no action was taken by the tribe or group.

   b. **Modern retribution**: Today, incarceration in prison is the principal form of retribution imposed on offenders. Although punishment in kind is supported to some degree, cruel and unusual punishment is forbidden by the United States Constitution. (What constitutes "cruel and unusual" punishment may vary with prevailing societal views. Thus, for example, capital punishment has been accepted at some places and times and prohibited at others.)

3. **Expiation:** Where the societal reaction to crime stresses expiation, the offender atones for his or her misdeeds by suffering. Like banishment and retribution, expiation is a traditional basis for punishment which is still commonly used today. The expiation function is most evident where punishment is made public or is imposed as a means of appeasing the public. In such cases, the punishment provides an outlet for the wrath of the community and gives the community a feeling of moral superiority.

4. **Deterrence:** Deterrence as a response to crime is designed to prevent a recurrence of criminal behavior. Specific deterrence is supposed to show particular offenders what will happen if *they* commit a certain offense again. General deterrence, in contrast, refers to the punishment or control of offenders for the purpose of showing *other* members of society what will happen to them if they violate the law. Underlying both kinds of deterrence is the assumption that failure to punish an offender may imply that the offense is condoned or tolerated.

   a. **Effect of deterrence uncertain:** Whether punishment for the purpose of deterrence is an effective means of thwarting crime is still a subject of controversy, especially in the case of general deterrence. It is difficult (if not impossible) to measure such effectiveness, since—among other reasons—one cannot measure behavior that has yet to occur. With respect to specific deterrence, capital punishment—the most drastic form—obviously prevents that particular offender from committing crimes in the future. The specific-deterrence value of other forms of punishment, however, is less certain.

   b. **Current popularity:** Despite these uncertainties, deterrence as a response to crime and criminals is enjoying renewed popularity at the present time. Many academicians, criminal justice personnel, lawmakers, journalists, and members of the general public have expressed confidence in the deterrent effect of punishment. These proponents generally argue that deterrence is most likely to be effective where punishment for criminal offenses is certain and alternatives to criminal behavior are made available to the offender.

5. **Rehabilitation:** Rehabilitation as a response to crime assumes that something is wrong with the offender or he or she would not be in trouble. Consequently, it is felt that society must first attempt to diagnose the problem or problems responsible for the criminal behavior and then correct or rehabilitate the offender.

   a. **Common techniques for rehabilitation:** Vocational training, education, and religious counseling have been important tools in the rehabilitation model; and both individual and group counseling services have been utilized in most treatment programs. In some programs, medical treatment in the form of psychotherapy, plastic surgery, chemotherapy, or psychosurgery has been used to enhance the offender's self-image and social standing in order to foster effective rehabilitation. In more recent times, biofeedback training has also been employed for the same purpose.

   b. **Basic goals of rehabilitation:** The foregoing types of treatment seek to correct the offender by constructive rehabilitation while at the same time protecting society by confining or supervising the offender during the period of rehabilitation. The treatment model also seeks to prevent or reduce crime by identifying potential criminals in advance and treating the sources of criminal behavior; and it regards any particular criminal act as relevant only if it has diagnostic value in the classification and treatment of offenders.

    c. **Criticism of rehabilitation approach:** The treatment model has come under attack from several quarters. Some critics focus on the theory of rehabilitation, some on the techniques employed, and some on both aspects. In general, however, these critics charge that the treatment model is based on fallacious assumptions about the nature and correction of crime, and that the practices employed under the model have resulted in highly arbitrary—and largely ineffective—treatment of offenders.

6. **Reintegration:** Reintegration as a response to criminal behavior involves helping offenders to develop more meaningful lives as law-abiding members of their communities. This approach has gained considerable support in recent years. In contrast to the treatment or rehabilitation model, which focuses on diagnosing and subsequently treating the "flaws" in individual offenders, reintegration emphasizes the *community* as the source of and the vehicle for positive change in offenders.

    a. **Basic techniques:** In the reintegration approach, attention is given to improving family life, employment opportunities, and other relevant aspects of the offender's existing situation; and in this connection, traditional counseling, psychotherapy, or other treatment may be utilized. However, primary emphasis is placed on the relationships and interactions of the offender with other members of the community. And since the community is deemed to play a major role in the prevention and control of criminal behavior, the corrections process may be called on to restructure social institutions in order to bring about desired changes in criminal offenders.

    b. **Foundations of probation and parole:** To a large extent, both the theory and the methods of modern community-based corrections—including probation and parole—are based on a reintegrationist approach to crime and criminal offenders.

B. IDEOLOGICAL BASES FOR SOCIETAL RESPONSES TO CRIME

In Western society, the responses to criminal behavior just discussed emanate from three underlying "revolutions" in criminological thought: the Classical School in the eighteenth century, the Positive School in the nineteenth century, and the Reintegrationist School in the twentieth century. Each of these schools of thought has provided an ideological basis for the societal response to crime—including the correctional practices of probation and parole. Hence, it is not surprising that debates concerning the need for change in corrections focus on philosophical issues as well as on policies and procedures.

1. **The Classical School:** The Classical School of criminology was established in the eighteenth century by Cesare Beccaria, an Italian, and Jeremy Bentham, an Englishman. It departed from the widespread assumption of that period that criminal or deviant behavior was caused by supernatural forces, replacing such assumptions with an integration of several philosophical theories widely shared during that period.

    a. **Philosophical roots of the Classical School:** The philosophical assumptions which formed the basis of the Classical School included free will, hedonism, rationalism, and the social contract theory of the state.

(1) **Free will:** According to the classical approach, free will is the capacity of an individual to choose a course of action without being influenced by external factors or forces.

(2) **Hedonism:** Similarly, hedonism was defined as the tendency of individuals to follow a course of action (or inaction) that would enable them to achieve pleasure or avoid pain.

(3) **Rationalism:** Rationalism, in the Classical system stressed that reason—rather than empiricism, authority, or spiritual revelation—was the primary basis for human action.

(4) **Social contract theory of the state:** The social contract theory postulated that each individual surrenders only enough of his or her liberty to make society viable. According to this view, laws are merely necessary conditions of the social contract; and punishment for violations of law should be imposed only to defend the individual's liberties from abuse by others.

b. **Perspective of the Classical School:** According to the Classical School, each individual had a free will, so a criminal acted of his own volition. Such behavior was attributable to rational rather than supernatural causes, and—under the social contract theory—the criminal was accountable to society just as society was responsible for protecting the rights of individuals. Since a criminal's choice of action (like that of other individuals) was based on hedonistic principles, the punishment assigned to each crime should ensure that the criminal received more pain from the punishment than he or she derived pleasure from commission of that crime. Penal codes thus were instruments of deterrence rather than retribution, and were to be clearly written and applied uniformly to all members of society. Finally, the guiding principle for *all* laws was held to be "the greatest good for the greatest number."

c. **Contributions of the Classical School:** The Classical School is the source of several principles of our modern criminal justice system, including the following:

(1) **Equal justice**—the belief that all people are subject to the law and should be treated as equals under the law, with the state viewed as "a nation of laws" rather than "a nation of men."

(2) **Codified statutes**—the requirement that criminal statutes be clearly stated in writing.

(3) **Speedy trial by jury**—the notion that accused persons should be able to have their cases heard by an impartial jury without unreasonable delay.

(4) **Defined punishment**—the requirement that the type of punishment applied for commission of a crime be established by code and applied in the same manner to all who commit that crime.

(5) **Humane punishment**—the rejection of arbitrary or excessively severe punishments, on the theory that the punishment should fit the crime.

d. **Criticisms of the Classical School:** At the same time, the Classical approach to criminology has been criticized on three basic grounds.

   (1) **"Treats the offense rather than the offender":** The Classical School focused on providing just and uniform punishment of offenders according to the crime committed, with the type and severity of the offense dictating the punishment meted out. However, critics contend that no two crimes and no two offenders are alike. Because motives, knowledge, circumstances, and available options may vary widely among offenders, these critics argue that a system which imposes punishment solely on the basis of the offense committed will result in substantial injustice in many cases. Moreover, it is argued that ostensibly uniform punishments may have an uneven (and unfair) impact when applied to offenders in different circumstances. For example, a $200 fine would hardly have the same effect on a millionaire that it would on a welfare recipient. For these reasons, critics of the Classical system argue that the societal response to crime must be individualized in order to achieve the goal of equal justice.

   (2) **"Encourages legal inflexibility":** The Classical School has also been criticized as promoting an attitude that laws are proper ends in themselves. The correct perspective, according to these critics, is that laws (including penal codes) are human creations which exist for the purpose of meeting certain needs of society. It is argued that this latter perspective encourages greater flexibility and permits the criminal justice system to be more responsive to changing societal attitudes and needs.

   (3) **"Promotes justice but neglects restoration":** Third, critics have noted that while the Classical School emphasized rational legal systems and uniform application of punishment, it did not deal with the restoration process—that is, the process of helping offenders to become useful, productive citizens. These critics contend that real justice for offenders and society cannot be achieved where the restoration process is largely ignored.

e. **Modern Neo-classical approach:** In more recent times, a modification of the original Classical system, known as the Neo-classical School, has emerged. This latter approach accepts the validity of mitigating or moderating circumstances, and adopts a modified view of the doctrine of free will. The degree to which an offender is responsible for his or her actions is considered in assigning punishment for a crime; and factors such as age, insanity, and intent are deemed relevant not only to assessment of criminal behavior but also to the proper treatment of offenders. The Neo-classical approach is evident in many of the proposed changes in corrections systems discussed in Chapter IX.

2. **The Positive School:** In the nineteenth century, another system of ideas emerged in Europe with the work of Lombroso, Garofalo, and Ferri of Italy. These ideas were formulated in what is now referred to as the Positive School of criminology. This approach reflected the perspective and methodology of the natural sciences and emphasized determinism in analyzing human behavior. According to the Positivists, behavior is determined by preexisting forces, just as the fall of an apple is determined by gravity. The effects of human heredity and environment were therefore given primary attention.

a. **Contributions of the Positive School:** The Positive School has contributed to modern criminology in at least two important respects: use of scientific methods, and emphasis on rehabilitation or treatment of offenders.

(1) **Scientific methods:** The present-day reliance on inductive methods, empirical data, and reexamination of theories and findings in the area of corrections all stem from the scientific approach of the Positive system.

(2) **Correctional practices:** The philosophical concepts of the Positive School also helped to foster a number of correctional policies currently in use.

(a) **Indeterminate sentencing:** Lombroso and other Positivists held that sentences should be flexible, since the amount of time needed for effective treatment varies from offender to offender.

(b) **Individualized treatment of offenders:** Since no two offenders are exactly alike, and since the reasons for and circumstances of offenses may also vary, the Positive School believed that treatment should be designed to meet the particular needs of each offender.

(c) **Classification of offenders:** In order to make treatment programs successful, the Positivists held, offenders should be classified according to their needs, interests, personalities, and capabilities.

(d) **Alternatives to incarceration:** Finally, Lombroso and other Positivists emphasized that alternatives to incarceration in prison should be used whenever possible. Among the alternatives suggested by the Positivists were victim compensation, labor, confinement at home, and the conditional sentence (which resembles modern probation). This view directly influenced modern community-based corrections programs, including probation and parole.

b. **Criticisms of the Positive School:** The Positive system has been criticized for failing to acknowledge the "personal responsibility" of the offender for his crime. By emphasizing treatment of the offender rather than the offense, Positivism allegedly encourages an unsound medical or rehabilitation model and generally results in an ineffective criminal justice system. In recent years, the prevalence of this criticism has increased and may well lead to certain modifications in correctional theory and practice.

3. **The Reintegrationist School:** The Reintegrationist approach to criminology stresses the role of the *community* as both a source of and an instrument for positive change in offenders. In this respect, it is a significant departure from both the Classical and Positive Schools and forms the basis for our present, community-oriented corrections approach (discussed below).

C. PRESENT SOCIETAL RESPONSES TO CRIME: COMMUNITY CORRECTIONS

Historically, penal institutions merely isolated prisoners from the mainstream of society until ordered to release them. Today, however, expectations for the corrections system are considerably higher: Both the public and corrections experts assume that, at minimum, offenders should be no worse for their correctional experience; and the hope is that offenders can reintegrate themselves into society as productive, law-abiding citizens. This view has resulted in an expansion of the perceived function of probation and parole, from a system of nominal supervision of the offender (with some casework counseling or therapy) to a program that focuses on the total circumstances of the offender and utilizes community resources to facilitate his or her reintegration into society.

1. **Perceived Need for Community Corrections**: The expectations just referred to have fostered a belief that, to be effective, a corrections program must be linked to the community in every phase of its operations. In turn, this has resulted in the formation of several types of community-based programs. Not all offenders can be dealt with in the community; and the protection of society should be a prime concern of correctional workers in any program. Nevertheless, community-based programs have proved to be a viable alternative to incarceration for juvenile and adult offenders in many cases.

2. **Basic Concepts in Community Corrections**: "Community corrections" refers to the placement of offenders in the community, under supervision. The offender may live at home, at a school, in a halfway house, with a foster family, or in a group living arrangement. This approach envisions a full range of alternatives to incarceration, as well as means of facilitating the successful reintegration of offenders into the community whether before or after release from a correctional institution. The system recognizes that offenders are subject to restraints: They are restricted as to where they may live, what they may do, and those with whom they may associate; they are regularly seen by probation or parole officers (or other supervisory agents); and they may be required to undergo psychotherapy or participate in a rehabilitation program. However, offenders are not isolated in confinement, and the hope is that they will respond to the support provided.

   a. **Goals of community-based corrections**: A community corrections program is designed to give the offender the chance to learn new skills, develop positive relationships and attitudes, and establish himself or herself in a noncriminal environment. Since few offenders are capable of handling such readjustments on their own, the correctional service must be able to assist the offender in obtaining necessary services and support for his or her productive reentry into society.

   b. **Advantages of community-based corrections**: A community corrections approach appears to have the following advantages over other systems in dealing with criminal behavior:

      (1) **Avoids harm of incarceration**: Incarceration tends to isolate offenders physically and psychologically—cutting them off from family, job, school, and other supportive influences, and increasing the probability that they will have an indelible "criminal" label. Successful reintegration is much more likely without the drawbacks of incarceration, and the community-based approach avoids these disadvantages.

      (2) **Provides financial saving**: One big advantage of community programs is the financial saving they can offer in comparison with other corrections approaches. When offenders are kept in the community instead of being institutionalized, the costs of incarceration are avoided and the offenders can remain employed—thereby enabling victims to be repaid and relieving society of the obligation to support the offenders' families.

      (3) **Emphasizes societal involvement in corrections process**: By their very nature,

community-based facilities tend to emphasize that all members of the community have a role to play in restoring offenders to useful citizenship.

(4) **Lowers recidivism rates**: One of the most serious problems confronting the corrections process is *recidivism*—the relapse of many offenders to a life of crime. Society must either prepare offenders for successful reentry as law-abiding citizens or be prepared to deal with the majority of them again as recidivists. Recidivism rates for community treatment programs are generally lower than those for institutions.

(5) **Promotes offender responsibility**: Community-based corrections places greater decision-making responsibility on offenders, since they are involved daily in community situations that require such decision making. In turn, offenders gain self-esteem when they find (with community support) that they can make responsible decisions. Prisons, in contrast, allow offenders little personal responsibility.

(6) **Offers positive role models**: Life in the community presents many more positive "role models" whom the offender can observe overcoming real-life difficulties and handling real-life situations on a daily basis. Other correctional modes, such as incarceration, offer very few behavior models worthy of emulation.

(7) **Affords positive reintegration experiences**: Community-based programs provide many opportunities for reintegrating the offender into the community. In contrast, there is considerable evidence that the institutional experience is brutalizing and destructive to those incarcerated. While imprisonment is temporary for most inmates, the isolation and alienation involved work against a successful reintegration into society.

(8) **Provides a realistic correctional test setting**: Just as the community provided the original setting for the offender's crime, it also provides the ultimate testing ground for the success of the rehabilitation process. And since community-based programs focus the rehabilitation process on reinvolving the offender in society, readjustment is more effective than with programs conducted in institutions.

(9) **Involves a more humanitarian approach to corrections**: Finally, the humanitarian nature of community-based corrections is one of the most important characteristics of this type of treatment. Subjecting anyone to incarceration means placing that person in physical jeopardy, drastically restricting his or her ability to find personal satisfaction, and reducing his or her self-esteem. Thus while incarceration will always be required in some cases, and the need for prisons will remain, offenders are more likely to benefit from community programs which remove the burdens of custody than they are from the "discipline" of prolonged incarceration.

3. **Role of Probation and Parole in Community Corrections—A Summary**: As noted previously, the dominant goal of community corrections is the successful reintegration of offenders into society. Probation and parole seek to accomplish this by providing supervision for offenders while protecting the public.

a. **Probation**: "Probation" refers to the conditional, supervised release of an offender into the community as an alternative to incarceration in a correctional institution.

b. **Parole:** "Parole" involves the conditional release into the community of a prisoner who has served part of a sentence in a correctional institution. Such release is usually supervised by an agency of the executive branch of government.

c. **Distinctions between probation and parole:** Perhaps the most useful bases for a comparison of probation and parole are responsibility for the decision process, incarceration experience, criminal records, adjustment needs, and societal reactions to probationers and parolees.

   (1) **Responsibility for decision process:** Probation is the responsibility of a trial court in the *judicial* branch of government. Parole is the responsibility of an agency in the *executive* branch (such as a state parole board).

   (2) **Incarceration experience:** An offender who is placed on parole has always served some time in a correctional institution. Persons given probation, however, usually have not served any sentence in a jail or prison.

   (3) **Criminal records**

      (a) **For parolees:** Parolees often have extensive criminal records, with convictions for serious offenses. In addition, the fact that they have been incarcerated may foster a "criminal" identification for such persons.

      (b) **For probationers:** Offenders placed on probation typically have less extensive criminal experience than parolees; and in some jurisdictions probation is available *only* to first offenders or to persons convicted of less serious offenses.

   (4) **Adjustment needs:** The adjustment needs of parolees and probationers can be quite different.

      (a) **Needs of parolees:** Release from prison into the community thrusts the parolee into a very different life situation. Incarceration in prison isolates or severely weakens the ties a prisoner has with family, friends, and work associates; and many paroled offenders find their family and employment situations quite different from what they were when they entered prison. Parolees therefore need to redefine old relationships, establish new ties, and find a place for themselves once again in the community. Moreover, parolees will be expected to take control of their lives and assume responsibility for themselves and their families—a much different situation from the prison environment, where most decisions affecting their lives were made for them.

      (b) **Needs of probationers:** By contrast, probationers usually have not been isolated from their families or the community. Since probation essentially involves "business as usual" for such offenders, they do not face the extensive adjustments required for parolees.

   (5) **Societal reactions**

      (a) **To parolees:** As a result of their incarceration in a prison or other institution, parolees suffer from the stigma of being "ex-cons." The public reacts to such labels; and the likelihood of rejection for those who have served time is greater than for those who have not. The readjustment of parolees to society is made more difficult by this distrust and rejection, which can affect such important areas of a parolee's life as his or her ability to obtain credit or satisfactory employment.

   (b) **To probationers:** Because probationers usually have not served time in an institution, they are less likely to be considered "ex-cons" or "criminals." Moreover, there is a common societal preconception that the offense committed by such a person cannot have been a serious one, since he or she "got probation."

d. **Factors contributing to confusion:** Despite the differences between probation and parole just described, there is a tendency to confuse the two concepts and to use the terms interchangeably. The principal reasons for this confusion appear to be improper usage of the terms by the news media, possible consolidated structuring of services, and certain overlapping policies and practices (such as "shock probation," "split sentences," or "bench parole").

   (1) **Confusion of terms by mass media:** Television and the press often use the terms "probation" and "parole" interchangeably in their news coverage. As a result, the general public may tend to view the two processes as being one and the same.

   (2) **Consolidated probation and parole systems:** In the federal system and in several states, supervision services for probation and parole are consolidated, both services being the responsibility of a single agency. Staff members in such consolidated systems may be referred to as probation or parole officers or by some other title, which may foster the impression that the objects of their supervision are likewise interchangeable.

   (3) **Correctional practices that "overlap" probation and parole:** Finally, certain types of corrections practices may overlap probation and parole, and this may lead to confusion of the two concepts.

      (a) **"Split sentences":** When an offender is given a split sentence, some jail time is required along with release on probation. Thus, split sentencing involves incarceration; and probationers subject thereto may be confused with parolees released after incarceration.

      (b) **"Shock probation":** Like split sentencing, shock probation involves spending some time in a jail or prison before being released on probation. As the term suggests, the purpose of such confinement is to "shock" the offender and promote a successful period of probation; but since these probationers have been incarcerated, they too may be confused with parolees.

      (c) **"Bench parole":** The term "bench parole" is a misnomer, since it is not a parole at all but a very mild form of probation involving a suspended sentence without supervision by a probation officer. Use of the term "parole," however, may cause the offender to be labeled a parolee rather than a probationer.

II. PROBATION: IN GENERAL

A. BASIC SCOPE AND FUNCTIONS OF PROBATION

1. **Scope of Probation:** The word "probation" is derived from the Latin word *probatio*, meaning a period of testing or furnishing proof of goodness.[1] Today, the term is used in any of four different contexts, to refer to a disposition, a status, a system or subsystem, or a process.[2]

   a. **Probation as a disposition:** When used in the context of a disposition, probation refers to the action of a court in suspending an offender's sentence and allowing him or her to remain in the community under supervision and subject to certain conditions.

      Example: An example of this use of the term probation is found in the following definition from the American Bar Association Project on Standards for Criminal Justice:

      > A sentence not involving confinement which imposes conditions and retains authority in the sentencing court to modify the conditions of sentence or to re-sentence the offender if he violates the conditions. Such a sentence should not involve or require suspension of the imposition or execution of any other sentence. . . . A sentence to probation should be treated as a final judgment for the purposes of appeal and similar procedural purposes.[3]

   b. **Probation as a status:** Probation may also refer to the legal position or status of a person sentenced to probation. The rights and duties of a probationer generally differ from those of a free citizen, an inmate, or a parolee.

   c. **Probation as a system or subsystem:** The term probation likewise may refer to the organization that processes those who have been placed on probation. In this sense, probation is a subsystem of corrections, which in turn is a subsystem of the criminal and juvenile systems.

   d. **Probation as a process:** Finally, probation may refer to the functions, activities, and services that characterize dealings among the courts, the probationer, and the community.

2. **Specific Functions of Probation Agencies:** Probation agencies provide a range of services to the courts, to offenders placed on probation, and to the community at large.

   a. **Services to the courts:** Probation agencies are sometimes referred to as the "eyes, ears, and legs" of the criminal and juvenile courts, owing to the wide variety of services performed by such agencies for the courts. Among the most important of these are intake services, preparation of reports, public relations work, coordination of services with related public and private agencies, surveillance, and investigative services.

      (1) **Intake services:** In juvenile probation, one or more members of the probation staff may have the responsibility of screening and making decisions regarding the processing of cases referred to the juvenile court by law enforcement agencies, schools, families, neighbors, and other agencies. (In some courts, these tasks are handled by detention personnel or by a legal services department.)

(2) **Preparation of reports:** In a juvenile probation case, a social history report is prepared by the probation officer and submitted to the court as an aid in arriving at an appropriate disposition of the case. With respect to adult offenders, a similar pre-sentence investigation report will be made by the probation officer if requested by the court. The extensiveness of such reports and the degree to which they are relied on by the court varies from jurisdiction to jurisdiction.

(3) **Surveillance of probationers:** Probation agencies are charged with the responsibility of ensuring that offenders placed on probation uphold the conditions of their release. In the event that excessive violations of these conditions or new offenses occur, it is the responsibility of the probation department to bring the matter to the attention of the court.

(4) **Miscellaneous services:** Depending on the jurisdiction involved, probation agencies may provide other services for the courts as well. Among such possible tasks are the following:

    (a) Ordering the arrest and detention of probationers who violate the conditions of their probation;

    (b) Evaluating alleged damage to the property of victims;

    (c) Coordinating court referrals to other agencies;

    (d) Administering detention release hearings;

    (e) Preparing statistical data and other periodic reports;

    (f) Delivering probationers to and from places of custody or incarceration;

    (g) Representing the court to the general public in probation matters.

b. **Services to probationers:** The supervision of probationers involves three interrelated elements: surveillance, community service brokerage, and direct services.

(1) **Surveillance:** Surveillance is the process of keeping in touch with a probationer to ensure that he or she adequately carries out the probation plan. In so doing, the probation agency provides individualized treatment and demonstrates to the probationer its concern that he or she not engage in future criminal or self-defeating behavior.

(2) **Community service brokerage:** Community service brokerage is the process of ascertaining and obtaining other community services required by the probationer or his or her family. Here, the probation officer acts as a mediator or advocate for the probationer-client, enlisting the aid of other agencies for employment, vocational training, medical care, and related assistance. The probation department coordinates such activities to ensure that the probationer and his or her family utilize the services effectively.

(3) **Direct services:** Probation departments likewise provide direct services to their

probationer-clients, of which counseling is perhaps the most important. The goal of counseling is to mobilize the probationer's abilities and potential to resolve personality problems and difficulties in his or her life situation—particularly those problems and difficulties that have contributed to past criminal behavior. In addition to counseling, the probation officer may provide such other direct services as role modeling and manipulation of the environment.

c. **Services to the community**: Besides assisting the courts and the probationer, probation departments offer services to the general public.

(1) **Educational and advocacy role of probation**: Probation agencies play a major role in informing the public of problems and needs in working with offenders. Utilizing the press and other media, the probation department can help to educate the community about its resources and shortcomings in this important task. And by participating in community planning and other organizing efforts, probation agencies can help the community to reintegrate offenders into society.

(2) **Protection of the public**: By effectively supervising probationers, probation departments fulfill their most important responsibility: the protection of the public. Probation is usually ordered in lieu of incarceration, and is granted conditionally on the assumption that it will not jeopardize the general public. Probation departments help to protect the public directly by controlling the behavior of the probationer, and indirectly by fostering his or her rehabilitation and reintegration into the community.

B. HISTORICAL DEVELOPMENT OF PROBATION

1. **Common-Law Antecedents of Probation**: In England and the early United States, several methods were developed to avoid the rigid application of harsh punishments to offenders. "Benefit of clergy," judicial reprieve, release of an offender on his or her own recognizance, bail, and the "filing" of cases were all used to suspend punishment subject to good behavior (though without supervision of offenders during the period of suspended sentence).

a. **Benefit of clergy**: Benefit of clergy was a privilege extended to the clergy (and later to all persons who could read), under which those convicted of a capital crime other than treason could obtain a hearing in the bishop's court. Being tried in an ecclesiastical court usually resulted in more lenient treatment than trial in a secular court, where the death sentence was commonplace. The offender was asked to quote a passage from the psalm *Miserere me* ("Have mercy on me") in order to qualify for benefit of clergy. Before long, illiterates had memorized the passage and thus could qualify for trials in a church court. Benefit of clergy was used in the American colonies prior to the Revolutionary War, and continued in England (at least for the aristocracy) until 1841.

b. **Judicial reprieve**: Another early form of relief was judicial reprieve, which involved a temporary stay on the imposition or carrying out of a sentence to allow time for the offender to apply for a pardon, or where the court was skeptical of the evidence presented. In some cases, judicial reprieve resulted in a permanent or indefinite suspension of sentence, although it is doubtful the device was ever intended to have this effect.

c. **Release on own recognizance**: Initially, recognizance was used as a device to prevent crime. People suspected of committing certain offenses would promise not to commit such crimes; and this "assurance to the public" became a recognizance or bond enforceable by the state if the conditions of the bond were not met. Later, recognizance was extended to persons who were actually arraigned for criminal offenses; but it was still used to ensure against recommission of the offense. The practice of *releasing* an offender on his or her own recognizance was approved by the Massachusetts legislature in 1836 for use with less serious offenses, and other states subsequently adopted similar procedures. In some states, sureties were required for release on recognizance, while in others no surety was required.

d. **Bail:** While some courts allowed an offender to be released on his own recognizance without sureties, they might also release a person on bail. Because sureties were involved, release on bail resulted in some degree of supervision and can be viewed as the precursor of probationary supervision.

e. **Filing of cases:** The device of "filing" a case originated in Massachusetts and consisted of suspending imposition of sentence on the consent of the defendant and the prosecutor after a guilty verdict. The suspension was subject to conditions set by the court; and the case could be reopened for sentencing at any time on request of the prosecutor or the defendant.

2. **Foundations of Modern Probation**

a. **The "father of probation"—John Augustus:** The modern concept of probation stems from the mid-nineteenth century visit of a bootmaker to a municipal court in Boston, Massachusetts. The bootmaker, John Augustus, had talked with an offender charged before that court with public drunkenness and had become convinced that the man could be reformed without being incarcerated. With the permission of the court, Augustus provided bail and the prisoner was released under Augustus' supervision. Soon Augustus was assisting many people in this capacity, utilizing a careful selection process and keeping detailed records of his supervision. His work helped to pave the way for subsequent legislative acceptance of the technique. Borrowing a term used to refer to novices in certain Protestant churches, John Augustus called his new procedure "probation."

Although Augustus' rehabilitative efforts were successful and he enjoyed the support of many judges, others in the criminal justice system—particularly clerks and policemen who lost fees they would otherwise have received for delivering offenders to the house of correction—were adamantly opposed to this approach. From the beginning, therefore, probation was controversial: It was strongly supported by some and bitterly resented by others.

b. **Early probation practices**

(1) **First paid probation officer:** In 1878, some twenty years after the death of John Augustus, probation was recognized by a Massachusetts statute authorizing the city of Boston to hire a paid probation officer (under the auspices of the supervisor of police). The statute permitted probation for offenders of either sex and of all ages whenever an offense appeared not to require punishment.

(2) **Statewide authorization of probation:** In 1880, another Massachusetts statute provided for the hiring of probation officers throughout the state. This early legislation

stipulated that probation officers could not be actively employed by a police department (a requirement commonly found in state statutes today). In the closing decade of the nineteenth century, several other states passed similar laws authorizing probation.[4]

c. **Legal challenge to probation**: From the beginning, the practice in probation was to suspend sentence and place the offender on probation instead. Unlike the common-law practices discussed previously in this chapter, which were intended as temporary and applicable only in specific cases, probation implied a permanent suspension of sentence for any offender who met the eligibility requirements. The legality of indefinite suspension of sentences was therefore brought into question. Critics maintained that there were no common-law precedents for indefinite suspensions, and that such suspensions encroached on the power of the executive branch to grant pardons and reprieves.

   (1) **Illegality of indefinite suspensions: the *Killits* decision**: The question of whether the courts had the power to grant indefinite suspensions of sentences was resolved in the so-called *Killits* case of 1916.[5] In this decision, the United States Supreme Court held that federal courts did *not* have the power to suspend indefinitely the imposition or execution of a sentence. While acknowledging that temporary suspensions of sentence often became indefinite as a result of judicial failure to act on the matter in question, the Court ruled that such practices did not constitute a legal precedent or otherwise give legitimacy to indefinite suspensions. Instead, the Court held that judges could not arbitrarily refuse to enforce the law by indefinitely suspending sentence, since to do so would interfere with both legislative and executive branch authority.

   (2) **Effect of *Killits* on probation**: Ironically, the decision in *Killits* had a *favorable* impact on probation, which spread rapidly throughout the country thereafter. Even though the Supreme Court had held that the judiciary could not unilaterally suspend sentences indefinitely, it had also ruled that the *legislature* could authorize the use of indefinite sentences by the courts. In other words, if indefinite sentences were permitted under statutes passed by the legislature, they were legal. By thus resolving the original dispute concerning court authority to order probation and providing an acceptable legal basis for the practice, the *Killits* decision was a positive influence on the development of probation.

d. **The growth of probation**: During the ten years following *Killits*, probation came to be authorized by many states and by the federal government. However, probation practices and organization differed among these various jurisdictions. Two states, Illinois and Minnesota, authorized probation only for juveniles; similarly, some other states made only certain types of offenders eligible to receive probation. States like Rhode Island organized probation on a statewide basis, whereas others such as Vermont set it up on a county-by-county basis.[6]

3. **Development of Federal Probation**: On several occasions prior to the *Killits* decision in 1916, Congress had tried to give federal judges the right to grant probation. In 1925, the National Probation Act was finally passed. This Act permitted each federal district court (with the exception of the District of Columbia) to hire one probation officer.

   a. In 1930, the provision allowing only one probation officer per district was removed; and probation officers were given some responsibility for the supervision of parolees. The Bureau of Prisons in the Department of Justice was assigned responsibility for coordinating probation in the federal system, with the U.S. Attorney General as chief administrator.

b. Responsibility for federal probation was ultimately transferred to the Administrative Office of the United States Courts after the creation of that office by Congress in 1939.[7]

4. **Development of Juvenile Probation**

a. **Early English practices:** Special consideration for the treatment of juveniles has long been the rule in England. Indeed, a guidebook prepared in the year 1630 for use by justices of the peace reveals the attention given to children before the English courts.[8] Among other practices, legal guardians were sometimes appointed to supervise children whose parents were deceased, incapacitated, or incompetent.

b. **Early practices in the United States:** In the United States, probation for juveniles initially developed as an alternative to incarceration in juvenile institutions, which themselves had been set up to provide special treatment for juvenile offenders. Although the intentions behind their development had been well-meaning for the most part, juvenile institutions eventually became little more than prisons for their youthful inmates. Private employers contracted for the labor of these inmates, and serious exploitation often resulted. Faced with these problems, states such as New York and Pennsylvania began to use placement in foster homes as a way of keeping children out of institutions.[9]

(1) **Establishment of juvenile courts:** A major development in the juvenile justice system occurred with the creation of the first juvenile court in Cook County (Chicago), Illinois, in 1899. The court was given jurisdiction over all offenders up to the age of sixteen, and had the power to appoint a probation officer in certain situations (for example, when a child was placed in a foster home).

(2) **Regular use of probation:** By 1945, every state had adopted juvenile courts;[10] and probation has become a common practice in all such courts.

5. **Development of Misdemeanant Probation:** The first probation statute in the United States (the 1880 law in Massachusetts) made no distinction between felons and misdemeanants with regard to eligibility for probation. The statute merely stipulated that probation should be reserved for those who could be reformed without punishment. Since that time, the development of probation services for misdemeanor offenders has varied widely among the states (see discussion below).

6. **Probation Practices Today: In Brief**

a. **Adult felony probation and juvenile probation on state level:** Laws authorizing probation services now exist in all fifty states and Puerto Rico, although this was not the case until 1967.[11] Authorization of probation services and their effective utilization are not one and the same thing, however. Many juvenile courts have inadequate or token probation services or lack any services at all; and even fewer probation services have been developed and utilized in adult criminal courts.

(1) Nevertheless, there has been a perceptible trend throughout the country toward an increased use of probation. A directory published in 1907 listed approximately 800 probation officers in the United States, most of whom were providing services to juvenile offenders By contrast, the 1966 Task Force Report on Corrections showed more than 6,000 juvenile probation officers and almost half that number of officers for adult felony offenders;[12] and these figures have continued to increase in recent years.

(2) Table 2.1 indicates the number of probationers under state and local supervision in 1975, by state.

b. **Misdemeanant probation:** Although misdemeanants are arrested for less serious offenses than felons, many knowledgeable observers believe that such offenders may have very serious problems and may require supervision even more than felons. At the present time, however, probation for misdemeanants varies widely among the states: Some have large, well-developed misdemeanant probation services, while others offer no supervision at all (relying instead on such devices as unsupervised bench parole).

c. **Federal probation:** From its inception in 1925, the federal probation system grew to include over 800 probation officers by the early 1970's. The federal system includes 190 offices serving ninety-one federal district courts in the fifty states, the District of Columbia, and Puerto Rico.[13] Federal probation officers also provide services to parolees, mandatory releasees, and juveniles who are tried in the federal courts (the federal system having no separate juvenile courts).

Figure 2.1 illustrates the categories of, and increases in, offenders under federal probationary supervision during a recent ten-year period.

C. ORGANIZATION OF PROBATION SERVICES

1. **Early Organization:** In the early years of development, the hiring of probation officers and the probation agency itself were functions of the court. This often resulted in several probation departments within the same city, and created problems of overlapping jurisdiction among the various departments. At the same time, many parts of the country—particularly sparsely populated rural areas—had no probation services at all. This haphazard provision of services helped to foster the trend toward statewide administration of probation, discussed later in this chapter.

2. **Present Variations in Organization:** No single pattern for probation services exists in this country. Instead, there are wide variations in the organization of probation agencies, stemming from differences in underlying laws, operating philosophy, clientele, departmental size, and locus of responsibility.

a. **Variations in underlying laws:** The laws establishing probation services have differed among the states, resulting in organizational structures that vary from state to state and (frequently) within the same state. Some statutes created statewide probation organizations, while others delegated probation services to districts or counties. Some statutes make probation a function of the executive branch of government, whereas others give the judicial branch responsibility for probation services.

Table 2.1

Number of Adult and Juvenile Probation Clients Under State and Local Supervision During 1975, by Sex and by State

State	Number of Probation Clients Under Supervision During 1975					
	Adult Probation			Juvenile Probation		
	Total	Male	Female	Total	Male	Female
TOTAL STATE AND LOCAL	1,363,225	1,182,612	180,613	668,769	509,861	158,808
ALABAMA	14,413	12,786	1,627	9,274	6,392	2,882
ALASKA	1,144	996	148	1,325	1,140	186
ARIZONA	11,562	10,325	1,237	4,888	3,997	891
ARKANSAS	2,480	1,986	494	7,315	5,430	1,885
CALIFORNIA	233,549	199,877	33,672	93,763	73,010	20,753
COLORADO	14,489	11,779	2,710	8,882	7,178	1,704
CONNECTICUT	31,141	26,015	5,126	1,886	1,418	388
DELAWARE	3,123	2,800	323	1,937	1,646	291
DISTRICT OF COLUMBIA	6,607	5,848	759	3,713	3,230	483
FLORIDA	39,724	34,827	4,897	26,956	21,246	5,710
GEORGIA	30,783	26,726	4,057	17,088	13,099	3,989
HAWAII	2,435	2,298	137	1,508	1,171	337
IDAHO	3,540	3,115	425	4,316	3,272	1,044
ILLINOIS	54,728	46,505	8,223	19,724	14,996	4,728
INDIANA	21,401	18,079	3,322	20,226	15,717	4,509
IOWA	6,400	5,731	669	12,186	8,943	3,243
KANSAS	6,825	5,842	983	15,439	10,944	4,495
KENTUCKY	5,499	4,916	583	5,410	4,289	1,121
LOUISIANA	14,379	12,658	1,721	10,840	8,609	2,231
MAINE	3,785	3,476	309	2,096	1,680	416
MARYLAND	48,358[1]	45,860	2,498	11,841	10,169	1,672
MASSACHUSETTS	96,258	85,271	10,988	19,255	19,365	3,890
MICHIGAN	66,417	56,592	9,825	27,560	20,353	7,207
MINNESOTA	20,006	17,146	2,860	15,527	11,946	3,581
MISSISSIPPI	4,391	3,385	1,006	12,363	8,465	3,898
MISSOURI	28,461	24,504	3,957	30,453	21,653	8,800
MONTANA	2,131	1,936	195	4,937	3,376	1,561
NEBRASKA	7,521	6,720	801	3,340	2,483	857
NEVADA	1,753	1,568	185	3,916	2,775	1,141
NEW HAMPSHIRE	4,025	3,518	507	1,858	1,498	360
NEW JERSEY	61,820	53,723	8,097	19,133	15,262	3,871
NEW MEXICO	7,833	6,507	1,326	3,501	2,728	777
NEW YORK	71,967	62,678	9,289	23,474	18,414	5,060
NORTH CAROLINA	55,780	47,404	8,376	12,286	8,635	3,651
NORTH DAKOTA	835	770	65	4,002	3,141	861
OHIO	54,392	45,619	8,773	29,603	21,943	7,660
OKLAHOMA	12,705	10,799	1,906	4,682	3,383	1,299
OREGON	17,434	14,559	2,875	13,748	10,252	3,496
PENNSYLVANIA	62,025	56,377	5,648	31,558	26,208	5,350
RHODE ISLAND	3,973	3,222	751	2,703	2,349	354
SOUTH CAROLINA	23,131	20,759	2,422	9,521	6,593	2,928
SOUTH DAKOTA	1,038	934	104	1,875	1,434	441
TENNESSEE	7,651	6,386	1,265	13,020	9,523	3,497
TEXAS	120,441	104,927	15,514	35,522	26,978	8,544
UTAH	6,147	5,100	1,047	3,172	2,696	476
VERMONT	4,809	4,325	484	431	385	46
VIRGINIA	14,966	13,357	1,609	14,930	11,338	3,592
WASHINGTON	23,759	20,310	3,449	20,208	14,081	6,127
WEST VIRGINIA	2,753	2,502	251	5,424	4,161	1,263
WISCONSIN	21,492	18,533	2,959	19,029	14,018	5,011
WYOMING	895	736	159	1,204	852	352

[1] The number of adults under probation supervision in Maryland does not include support cases.

Source: U.S. Department of Justice, Law Enforcement Assistance Administration, *State and Local Probation and Parole Systems* No. SD-P-1 (Washington, D.C.: U.S. Government Printing Office, 1978), p. 38.

Figure 2.1

Persons Under Supervision of the Federal Probation Service, by Type of Supervision, on June 30, 1967–77

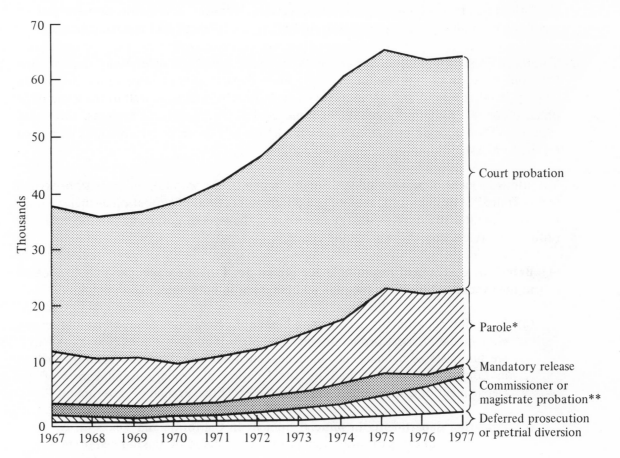

*Indicates military parole and special parole
**The Federal Magistrates Act came into full effect as of July 1, 1971

Source: Administrative Office of the United States Courts, *The United States Courts: A Pictorial Summary for the Twelve Month Period Ended June 30, 1977* (Washington, D.C.: Administrative Office of the United States Courts, 1977), p. 20.

b. **Variations in philosophy:** Philosophies of probation administration likewi~ one probation department to another. In some departments, the law-~ tion of probation is heavily emphasized, whereas other departme purpose as the rehabilitation or treatment of offenders. Many de their basic purpose is to reintegrate offenders into the communi embrace a combination of these philosophies.

c. **Variations in clientele:** Likewise, probation departments vary in the ~ serve. Some departments are responsible only for juveniles; others ser still others handle only misdemeanants. In certain instances, a single responsible for all types of probationers—juveniles, adult felons, ar

d. **Variations in size:** Probation departments also vary greatly i~ have only one or two probation officers, while department~ employ hundreds of officers. Variations in size are attributabic ~ organization of probation services: In some centrally administered sysic.. state may form a single probation "department"; while other systems may be orga... on the local level.

e. **Variations in locus of responsibility:** Finally, much of the variation in probation services in the United States can be traced to the differing locations of probation agencies within the governmental structure. Both the branch and the level of government responsible for probation services vary throughout the country.

(1) **Branch of government responsible for probation:** Probation agencies may be located in the executive branch, in the judicial branch, or in both branches.

(a) **Probation departments in executive branch:** In New York State, all probation services including local probation agencies (with the exception of New York City), are administered by an agency of the executive branch. Similarly, adult probation in Louisiana is administered by the Division of Probation and Parole of the Department of Corrections, located in the executive branch of government.

(b) **Probation departments in judicial branch:** In California and Texas, in contrast, services for all types of probationers are administered by the judicial branch.

(c) **Probation departments located in both branches:** Both the judicial and executive branches of government have responsibility for certain aspects of the probation system in Ohio. Juvenile probation is administered locally by the judicial branch; but the state program which funds juvenile probation departments is administered by the executive branch. Adult probation services are administered by both the state and the locality: Local courts may establish and provide their own services (as is the case of Cincinnati), or a state agency in the executive branch may be called on to provide services to the local courts. And where adult services are provided by the locality, both the executive and judicial branches of government are involved, in that county commissioners and judges of the court of common pleas must agree on the hiring of employees for the probation department. This illustrates the complexity of probation organization currently found in the United States.[14]

(2) **Level of government responsible for probation**: Perhaps the chief reason for variation and duplication of probation services is the fact that such services are provided at both the state and local levels of government.

(a) **Probation organized on local level**

1) **Small departments**: In departments with less than a dozen officers, the organizational structure is relatively simple. The administrative personnel may consist of a chief probation officer and one or two assistants, with a support staff including an office manager, secretaries, a bookkeeper, and a fiscal manager. The probation staff may work with volunteers and, in such small departments, will typically perform a wide range of investigative and supervisory tasks.

2) **Large departments**: Larger probation departments exhibit a greater degree of bureaucratization and specialization than do small departments. These larger departments may be separated into several different branches; and the larger the department, the more specialized and formally defined these branches are likely to be.

a) One branch in a large probation department may specialize in providing *field services*, such as investigation of referrals and supervision of probationers.

b) Another branch may specialize in providing *institutional services*, such as operation of county-owned detention centers and community-based treatment facilities.

c) Still another specialized branch in large departments may be primarily responsible for *administrative services*. This branch would be concerned with planning, coordinating, and evaluating service operations for the department as a whole.

d) Finally, specialized branches of a large probation department may be established to deal with such areas as misdemeanant probation, intake, investigation, supervision, and medical and psychiatric services.

(b) **Statewide organization of probation**

1) **Adult probation services**: Historically, probation services for adults were organized on a statewide basis; but that pattern is much less common today. In 1976, twenty-six states had statewide probation systems for adults, twenty-two states had a combination of state and local organization, and three had locally organized adult services.

2) **Juvenile probation services**: By contrast, juvenile probation services in 1976 were state-administered in twenty states, were administered by both state and local agencies in twenty-one states, and were exclusively a local function in ten states.[15]

(3) **Summary of distribution of responsibility for probation services:** Tables 2.2 and 2.3 indicate the distribution of responsibility for adult and juvenile probation services by branch and level of government for the fifty states and Puerto Rico. These tables illustrate the wide variations in locus of responsibility referred to previously.

3. **Proper Place for Probation in Governmental Structure**

   a. **Level of government—local or state:** Persuasive arguments can be made on both sides concerning the relative advantages of local or statewide administration of probation services.

      (1) **Advantages of local administration:** The basic arguments favoring local administration of probation are as follows:

         (a) **Better community reception for agency:** Locally controlled and administered probation agencies are more likely to be accepted as part of the local community. This is especially true where the community tends to be suspicious of a centralized and distant state government.

         (b) **Increased staff identification with community and its needs:** Similarly, it is argued that employees in a locally administered probation department are more likely to identify with the local communities than the staff of a state-administered agency. This argument assumes that personnel in a local department are likely to be hired from that community rather than transferred from a central state office, and that—being local residents—they will have greater knowledge of and access to local resources. Empirical evidence suggests that this is often the case—that even very competent and professional "outsiders" who are placed in a community by a state-administered probation program may have difficulty relating to local resources and needs. An example would be the newly graduated probation officer from a rural background assigned to a large metropolitan department (or vice versa).

         (c) **Greater flexibility of probation structures:** Third, it is argued that smaller, locally controlled and locally administered probation departments are less subject to rigid, uniform structures and policies than statewide probation systems, and are thus able to achieve more flexibility and creativity in their service programs. The contention is that local departments need sufficient independence in order to develop dynamic leadership and meet specific local needs.

      (2) **Advantages of statewide probation:** Proponents of statewide probation systems make some persuasive arguments for organization at that level.

         (a) **Increased uniformity of probation services:** First, it is argued that greater uniformity in services can be assured where probation administration is centralized statewide. The correctional philosophy, policies, and procedures behind probation are more likely to be articulated in a state system; and the large, unitary nature of such a system makes the probation agency more visible and thus more accountable to the public.

            1) **Past service problems in locally administered systems:** Under local probation

Table 2.2

State Distribution of Responsibility for the Adult Probation Function by Level(s) and Branch(es) of Government on September 1, 1976

Responsible Branch(es) of Government	Total States	Responsible Level(s) of Government		
		State only	Local only	State and local
Total States	51	26	3	22
Executive only	23	22	–	1
Judicial only	7	1	3	3
Executive and judicial	21	3	–	18

–Represents zero.

Table 2.3

State Distribution of Responsibility for the Juvenile Probation Function by Level(s) and Branch(es) of Government on September 1, 1976

Responsible Branch(es) of Government	Total States	Responsible Level(s) of Government		
		State only	Local only	State and local
Total States	51	20	10	21
Executive only	10	9	–	1
Judicial only	25	9	10	6
Executive and judicial	16	2	–	14

–Represents zero.

Source: Bureau of the Census, National Criminal Justice Information and Statistics Service, *State and Local Probation and Parole Systems* (Washington, D.C.: U.S. Government Printing Office, 1978), p. 103.

systems, it has been commonplace to find more than one probation department providing services in a single area of a state while other large sections of the state had no probation service. In sparsely populated rural areas, probation services often have been handled by the county sheriff; and "supervision" of probationers frequently amounted to having the probationer sign in by mail once a month. Small populations, coupled with small budgets and large geographic areas, intensified these problems and discouraged the development of effective local probation services.

2) **Continuing service problems in local systems:** Even today, problems in service coordination and quality tend to plague locally administered probation programs. Some of these problems can be traced to the wide disparities in population and resources within a given state. Texas is a case in point: Some of the nation's wealthiest and most populous counties, together with some of its poorest and least populated counties, are found within the borders of that state. Other problems in local services may stem from "accidents of geography." In Milford, Ohio, for example, the county line runs through the middle of town, so that offenders on one side of a street may be sent to a metropolitan court in Cincinnati while those on the other side of the street are sent to a suburban-rural county court in Batavia. And differing local traditions and cultures may result in further variations in probation services.

3) **Superiority of statewide system in handling problems:** The mere fact that a probation system is administered on a statewide basis will not eliminate all problems caused by the types of intrastate variations just discussed (and of course cannot compensate for such differences existing between states). However, such disparities are more likely to be handled effectively in a statewide system, since it can be organized around local needs with appropriate adjustments in staff size and resources while maintaining greater uniformity of service and a more flexible use of personnel and funds.

(b) **Better auxiliary services:** With its larger scope and budget, a statewide program is also in a better position to perform necessary auxiliary functions of the probation system. For example, collection of statistics, recruitment, education and training of staff, management of various community-based treatment programs, and research and development are difficult to accomplish in a system of loosely organized local probation departments; but they can be carried out effectively in a statewide program.

(c) **Greater professionalism of probation services:** It is argued that statewide probation systems encourage professionalization of the probation function among agency personnel. In local systems, probation personnel are more likely to see themselves as employees of their particular department and to identify exclusively with its needs, resources, and problems. This in turn can lead to interdepartmental rivalries pitting city against city, rural areas against urban, and the like. Such parochial attitudes, it is asserted, are less likely to develop in a statewide system where all staff members are identified with the same organization and there is a greater likelihood that probation officers will perceive themselves as professionals who happen to be working in a given department (rather than as employees of a particular department).

(d) **Less local political interference:** Finally, proponents of statewide probation systems contend that such systems offer more effective services because local political forces cannot exert the same influence and control as they can on locally controlled departments. In many cases, it is argued, programs have been implemented, staffs hired, and other services performed which would not have occurred had it been necessary to contend with and obtain the approval of local political leaders.[16]

b. **Branch of government—judicial or executive:** As noted previously, probation services may be administered by agencies located in the judicial or the executive branch of the government or, in certain circumstances, in both of these branches. Historically, the local court tended to be responsible for administering probation services; and to a large extent this is still true in juvenile probation. However, adult probation services are being administered more and more by agencies of the executive branch, especially where such services have been merged with parole administration. The National Advisory Commission on Criminal Justice Standards and Goals[17] has presented the following arguments on the respective merits of judicial and executive branch responsibility for probation:

(1) **Arguments favoring location in judicial branch**

(a) **Makes probation more responsive to courts:** If probation departments were located in the judicial branch, they would be more responsive to court direction. Throughout the probation process, the court could offer guidance to probation workers and take corrective action when particular policies were not followed or proved to be ineffective.

(b) **Automatic feedback mechanism:** Location in the judicial branch of government would likewise provide the judiciary with automatic feedback on the effectiveness of its case dispositions, through reports filed by the probation staff. Judges, it is felt, may give more weight to reports from staff members within the court system than to reports from an outside agency.

(c) **Greater awareness of required resources:** Courts have a greater awareness of the resources needed for effective probation services, and may therefore become advocates for their staffs in obtaining such resources.

(d) **Increased use of pretrial diversion:** Increased use of pretrial diversion may also result from placement of probation services in the judicial branch. Courts have not been inclined to transfer authority and thus may place more stringent limits on the discretion of nonjudicial personnel to release or divert offenders than they would on a judicial agency.

(2) **Arguments opposing location in judicial branch**

(a) **Judges as administrators:** When probation departments are located in the judicial branch, judges frequently become administrators of probation services—a role for which they are usually ill-equipped.

(b) **External priorities for staff:** When probation is administered from within the judicial system, the department staff may well give priority to providing services to the courts rather than to probationers (in, for example, issuing summonses and serving subpoenas). This may reflect the fact that courts are adjudicatory rather than service-oriented bodies, and that probation departments located within the judicial framework are likely to remain subservient to the court rather than developing identities of their own.

(3) **Arguments favoring location in executive branch**: In addition to the foregoing arguments against locating probation services in the judicial branch, there are arguments in favor of placing such services in the executive branch:

(a) **Improved coordination and functional integration**: All other subsystems for carrying out court-ordered dispositions of offenders (for example, prisons) are located within the executive branch of government. Thus, closer coordination and integration of probation with other correctional activities could be achieved by a common organizational base, particularly in the case of community-based corrections programs. Job mobility for personnel would also be enhanced if these related functions were joined administratively.

(b) **Improved coordination with social service agencies**: The executive branch likewise contains those service agencies allied with probation, including social and rehabilitation services, medical services, employment services, education, and housing. When probation is located in the executive branch, the opportunities for coordination, joint projects, and comprehensive planning among these various agencies are increased.

(c) **Improved distribution of resources**: Regardless of whether probation is located in the judicial or the executive branch, decisions involving allocation of resources and establishment of priorities are made by the executive branch. That branch initiates requests for appropriation of funds to the appropriate legislative body (local or state) and thereby sets priorities for the allocation of limited tax dollars. When probation is included in the total correctional system, more rational decisions about the best distribution of resources can thus be made.

(d) **Strengthened bargaining position**: Finally, probation administrators may be better able to negotiate their requests for funds and resources if they are part of the executive branch. When probation departments are located in the judicial branch, the judge rather than the probation administrator must present and negotiate the budget request; and this is not a role traditionally undertaken by the judiciary.

D. BASIC POSITIONS IN PROBATION DEPARTMENTS

Except in very small programs, a division of labor exists in most probation departments. The number and degree of specialization of probation personnel will vary, depending on factors such as size, range of tasks, and bureaucratic complexity. However, the following basic positions (and roles) are common to virtually all departments.

1. **Chief Probation Officer**: In any department with more than one professional on the payroll, there will be a chief probation officer or a position with some similar title. The chief pro-

bation officer typically has a wide variety of tasks, but may be expected to play a major role in hiring and promotion, training, supervision, administration, and public relations.

a. **Hiring and promotion**: The chief will play the leading role in appointment of assistants and other employees to perform the professional, clerical, and other work of the agency; and in some instances, he or she may assign volunteer workers to such tasks as well. The chief officer likewise initiates such personnel actions as promotions, discharges, and disciplinary measures.

b. **Training**: The chief officer has a guiding hand in the development and evaluation of in-service training programs for all staff members and volunteer probation workers. In this connection, he or she will review staff evaluations to determine training needs and see to it that programs to meet these needs are implemented.

c. **Supervision**: The chief probation officer also has overall responsibility for supervising and coordinating programs and activities within the department. Among other tasks of a supervisory nature, the chief studies and implements production schedules, estimates time requirements for job assignments, and analyzes and helps to resolve work- and grievance-related problems. Moreover, the chief fosters good morale and productivity throughout the department.

d. **Administration**: In discharging his or her administrative responsibilities, the chief probation officer is concerned with measures that will help achieve the overall goals of the department. This normally involves the chief officer in developing and implementing administrative procedures relating to personnel, staff development, training, fiscal and budgetary matters, and physical facilities. The chief must interpret departmental policies, job orders, and assignments to the staff and must ensure that department policies comply with acceptable standards. In performing these tasks, the chief confers with staff supervisors to coordinate the activities of individual sections within the department. (In smaller departments, the chief is likely to confer directly with some or all of the staff.)

e. **Public relations**: A final and very important responsibility of the chief probation officer is to maintain effective relationships with other agencies and organizations, as well as with the general public. Such public relations efforts are necessary if the department is to obtain the aid and resources of the community in achieving its goals.

2. **Assistant Chief Probation Officer**: Many departments will have an assistant chief probation officer or assistant director, who may be called on to perform a wide assortment of tasks (including standing in for the chief probation officer during the latter's absence from the department). While the duties of this position vary with departmental size, management design, and other factors, the assistant chief usually has responsibilities in coordinating volunteer programs and administering the department.

a. **Coordinating volunteer programs**: In many departments, the assistant chief probation officer manages the overall volunteer program. Tasks in this area include directing and coordinating the work of unpaid volunteer probation workers from the community and of volunteer agencies.

b. **Administrative responsibilities**: As an aide to the chief probation officer, the assistant chief is also called on to perform a variety of tasks in administering the department. He or she may collect statistical data and other information necessary to management of the agency; and he or she may be responsible for ensuring that department policies and procedures are followed by agency personnel.

3. **Supervisor:** As the title implies, a supervisor oversees the professional and clerical staff of the department—a job that requires the exercise of mature, independent judgment. Since this is a middle-management position, many supervisors have had firsthand experience as probation officers. Their duties generally include some or all of the following tasks:

    a. **Review of pre-sentence investigations:** The supervisor usually assumes overall responsibility for the pre-sentence investigations conducted by probation officers. In carrying out this responsibility, the supervisor is expected to provide advice and guidance, as well as quality control, in the preparation of pre-sentence reports.

    b. **Assignment of cases:** A supervisor usually has the responsibility of assigning client cases to the paid professional and volunteer probation staffs or to supervision teams.

    c. **Other responsibilities:** The supervisor also plays a leading role in training new and in-service probation officers, assistants, interns, and volunteers; and he or she is expected to assist, supervise, and help to evaluate all phases of work in the department.

4. **Probation Officer:** The work of the probation officer is central to the purpose of the agency, in that most contacts between the department and its probationer-clients occur through the officer in the form of investigation, direct services, and supervision. The nature of the probation officer's duties varies with the size of the department and with the division of labor within it. However, most officers have one or more of the following responsibilities:

    a. **Investigative tasks:** In at least some departments, the probation officer is required to prepare an initial investigatory report on each client (referred to as a *pre-sentence investigation report* in adult probation and as a *social history report* in juvenile probation). The purpose of this report is to aid the court in the disposition of the client's case. During the course of supervising clients, the probation officer may make other investigative reports as a matter of routine or when ordered to do so by the court.

    b. **Direct services:** The probation officer also provides aid and counseling to each client. Such direct services may be on a one-to-one basis; or the officer may work with clients in group settings or as one member of a team of professional and volunteer staff members. The officer also helps to coordinate community services and resources for the benefit of clients.

    c. **Surveillance responsibilities:** A third and major responsibility of the probation officer is to protect the public. Among other things, the officer keeps a watchful eye on his clients, reports violations of probation, and seeks to have probation revoked where this is warranted. In performing such tasks, the probation officer serves the dual purpose of helping his or her clients keep the terms of their probation and protecting the community.

NOTES

[1] *The Random House College Dictionary.* New York: Random House, 1973.

[2] National Advisory Commission on Criminal Justice Standards and Goals, "Probation, National Standards and Goals," *Corrections* (Washington, D.C.: U.S. Government Printing Office, 1973), pp. 311-40.

[3] American Bar Association Project on Standards for Criminal Justice, *Standards Relating to Probation* (New York: Institute of Judicial Administration, 1970), p. 9.

[4] United Nations Department of Social Affairs, *Probation and Related Measures* (E/CN/5/230 New York, 1951), pp. 15-42.

[5] *Ex parte United States*, 242 U.S. 27, 37, S. Ct. 72, 61 L. Ed. 129 (1916).

[6] United States Department of Justice, *Attorney General's Survey of Release Procedures*, Volume I, Digest (Washington, D.C.: U.S. Government Printing Office, 1939).

[7] Merrill A. Smith, *As a Matter of Fact . . . An Introduction to Federal Probation* (Washington, D.C.: The Federal Judicial Center, January 1973), pp. 1-9.

[8] See Frederic L. Faust and Paul J. Brantingham, *Juvenile Justice Philosophy* (St. Paul, Minn.: West, 1974), p. 44.

[9] *Ibid.*, p. 62.

[10] Herbert A. Bloch and Frank T. Flynn, *Delinquency* (New York: Random House, 1956), p. 315.

[11] David Dressler, *Practice and Theory of Probation and Parole*, 2nd ed. (New York: Columbia University Press, 1969), p. 28.

[12] President's Commission on Crime and Administration of Justice, *Task Force Report: Corrections* (Washington, D.C.: U.S. Government Printing Office, 1966), p. 27.

[13] Smith, pp. 1-9.

[14] National Advisory Commission on Criminal Justice Standards and Goals, pp. 313-14.

[15] Bureau of the Census, Governments Division, *State and Local Probation and Parole Systems.* Prepared for the United States Department of Justice, Law Enforcement Assistance Administration (Washington, D.C.: U.S. Government Printing Office, 1978), p. 103.

[16] National Advisory Commission on Criminal Justice Standards and Goals, pp. 315-16.

[17] *Ibid.*, pp. 313-14.

III. THE DECISION-MAKING PROCESS IN PROBATION

The actual decision regarding a grant of probation (and the terms thereof) is the responsibility of the trial court. However, such decisions are made within sentencing boundaries and often are directed or aided by pre-sentence investigations. The probation officer thus plays a major role in the decision-making process by conducting pre-sentence investigations and preparing probation plans for offenders.

A. ROLE OF THE TRIAL COURT

It is the function of the trial court to arrive at an appropriate disposition for a convicted criminal offender. In some cases a fine will suffice; at other times, incarceration will be necessary; and in still other cases, probation may be warranted. In certain cases of the last variety, the offender receives a prison sentence which is then suspended in whole or in part, the offender being placed on probation rather than serving time in prison. On other occasions, probation (with no suspended sentence) is the sole disposition of the court.

Whenever an offender receives probation, the court must set the terms of probation—usually conditions to which the offender must assent in writing. The court may spell out such terms in detail, or it may delegate the task to the probation officer, subject to certain guidelines. In the latter situation, the court will order the offender to obey the rules and conditions established by the probation officer.

1. **Effect of Eligibility Statutes:** Although the courts decide whether or not to grant probation, this decision must be made within the limits of statutes governing eligibility for probation. These statutes vary considerably from state to state. In some jurisdictions, any offender can be considered for probation, while in other jurisdictions those persons convicted of certain offenses (for example, violent crimes) are not eligible.

2. **No "Right" to Probation:** It should also be noted that mere eligibility for probation under the applicable statute does not give the offender a *right* to be placed on probation. The granting or withholding of probation (assuming eligibility) is a matter for the discretion of the trial court.

3. **Aids to Court in Decision-Making Process:** In determining whether to grant probation, the court must decide what course of action is in the best interests of both the offender and society at large. This requires answering questions such as whether the offender is too dangerous to be released into the community, whether incarceration would be helpful or even more damaging to the offender, whether the offender's personal and social situation is amenable to probation, and what impact the decision to grant or withhold probation may have on the offender, his or her family, the criminal justice system, and the general public. The trial judge has numerous other responsibilities and cannot personally research each sentencing matter in detail. Consequently, the court relies to a large extent on two sources of information: sentencing guidelines and the pre-sentence investigation report.

   a. **Sentencing guidelines:** Guidelines for sentencing involve a more or less standardized evaluation of offenders based on such factors as type of offense and prior record of the offender. Figure 3.1 illustrates one type of guideline, designed to predict the likelihood of successful probation.

Figure 3.1

Predictive Model:
Likelihood of Probation Success

California Form 61-B

TO OBTAIN RAW SCORES:

	If	*Add*	
A.	Arrest-free five or more years	16	____
	No history of any opiate use	13	____
	Not checks or burglary (subject offense)	13	____
B.	Age at subject offense times .6		____
	21 is added for all persons		_21_
C.	Subtotal: A + B		____
			____
D.	Aliases: –3 times number		____
E.	Prior known incarcerations:		
	–5 times number		____
F.	Subtotal: D + E		____
			____
G.	Score: Subtract F from C		____
			____

Rate on a Scale of 1–100

Source: Taken from Comptroller General's Report to Congress, *State County Probation Systems in Crisis* (Washington, D.C., 1976), p. 133.

Sentencing guidelines are necessarily general, which means that the court still has considerable discretion in most probation decisions and will rely extensively on reports from the probation officer. This increases the significance of the pre-sentence investigation report (below) in such decisions.

b. **Pre-sentence investigation report:** The probation officer's pre-sentence investigation (PSI) is a primary tool of the court in deciding for or against probation. Moreover, where the disposition is to order probation, the information contained in the PSI report helps the court to impose terms and conditions of probation that are realistic and appropriate to the particular offender involved.

B. ROLE OF THE PROBATION OFFICER

The probation officer plays a vital role in the decision-making process by providing the court with information about the offender. Even when such information is minimal and is supplied through informal communications between the trial judge and the probation officer, it will be used in all situations required by law or ordered by the court.

1. **The Pre-Sentence Investigation Report:** Some departments have staff members who specialize in conducting the PSI. Usually, however, the probation officer who would supervise the offender if probation were granted also prepares the PSI report.

   a. **General purpose of PSI:** The main purpose of a pre-sentence investigation is to provide insights and factual information about the offender as an aid to the court in making an appropriate disposition. The offender's personality, problems, strengths and weaknesses, and general life situation are explored. The pre-sentence investigation provides valuable information about the offender, his or her family and social relationships, criminal experiences and inclinations, school or occupational interests, capabilities, and achievements. In sum, it attempts to gather and interpret all information relevant to granting or denying probation and rehabilitating the offender.

   b. **Extent to which PSI is used:** Use of pre-sentence investigations varies from jurisdiction to jurisdiction, especially by the type of probation services involved.

      (1) **Adult probation:** The President's Commission on Law Enforcement and Administration of Justice concluded that approximately one-fourth of the states require a pre-sentence report for crimes punishable by more than one year of imprisonment. In the federal system and in most other states, the court has discretion to order or not to order a pre-sentence investigation.[1]

      (2) **Juvenile probation:** In juvenile courts, a social history—the equivalent of the pre-sentence investigation report used in adult cases—is used as an aid in making dispositions on probation. Where juvenile cases are heard by a judge, social histories are routinely ordered and supplied to the court. It should be noted, however, that only a fraction of juvenile cases are disposed of by judges. Many such cases are handled by court-appointed referees, intake officers, or even probation officers; and in these situations a social history may or may not be utilized.

      (3) **Misdemeanant probation:** PSI's are seldom used in misdemeanant probation. When

such investigations are made, the reports tend to be shorter than those prepared in adult felony or juvenile cases.

c. **Sources of information:** The information included in a pre-sentence investigation report is obtained from interviews with the offender, members of his or her family, past and present employers, officials of school and other social agencies, and from law-enforcement reports. In some cases, psychiatric or other medical reports may be consulted; and the offender's friends, codefendants, or clergyman may be interviewed. All too often, however, the heavy caseloads of probation officers mean that PSI reports are based on interviews with the offender and whatever corroborating evidence is easily accessible.

d. **Scope of investigation:** The content of pre-sentence investigations may vary somewhat, but generally includes relevant information about the offender, his or her offense, family and other significant social relationships, lifestyle, and future plans. Depending on the circumstances of the case, certain of these areas may be examined more extensively than others.

e. **Contents of PSI report:** The format of PSI reports also varies somewhat. However, the following topics are covered in most such reports:

(1) **Offender and court data**

(a) **Data on offender ("face sheet"):** Basic information regarding the offender—for example, legal name and aliases, address, telephone number, sex, and age—is set out in the first section of the report.

(b) **Data on offense:** This section includes a brief description of the alleged present offense and a brief listing of prior arrests. Such information is set forth in more detail in the "Arrest Record" section, below.

(c) **Agency data:** Basic agency data in the report includes the case docket number, date of probation, names of prosecuting and defense attorneys, any other court cases pending, and the offender's identifying numbers (if any) with the FBI and state or local law-enforcement agencies.

(2) **Present and past arrest record**

(a) **Present offense:** This section describes the facts and circumstances surrounding the offense. Where, when, and how the offense occurred may be important factors in deciding on an appropriate disposition; and the physical and mental condition of the offender at the time of the offense may also be relevant.

(b) **Past arrests and convictions:** A review of the offender's past criminal experiences can be useful in assessing the degree of commitment to a criminal lifestyle. The probation officer compiling the report will want to note patterns suggesting that the offender is an incidental lawbreaker, on the one hand, or a professional, compulsive, or sociopathic offender, on the other. Many experts regard past criminal history as one of the most reliable factors in predicting the chances for successful completion of probation.

(3) **Defendant's version of the offense**: The defendant's own version of the offense in question may reveal his or her attitudes toward the offense, the victim, the police, and others involved in his or her offense, arrest, and conviction. Hence, it can provide considerable insight into the degree to which the offender accepts responsibility for his or her present difficulties.

(4) **Family history and interaction**: For all but a very few offenders, the family is the primary group and a major (if not the most important) socializing agent in their lives. Therefore, information on family members, size and birth order of family, and patterns of interaction among family members may shed light on the character of the offender and the circumstances surrounding the offense. In some cases, other close associates of the offender, such as neighbors and friends, may provide valuable information in this area.

(5) **Education**: A detailed report of the defendant's educational background is most important in the case of juvenile or young adult offenders. Where policy permits, school officials are asked for information concerning the offender's behavior, health, intelligence, and achievement.

Note: Accurate school records are often difficult to obtain, even for young offenders; and the problem increases with older offenders. For most older adults, therefore, the time and effort otherwise required to obtain school records would be better spent in gathering more current information.

(6) **Employment**: Like past criminal activity, an offender's employment history is often a key predictor of whether he or she will complete probation. The employment history indicates such factors as stability, sense of responsibility, and ability to remain in long-term work relationships with others; therefore, it can reveal much about the offender's personality as well as catalogue his or her work training, experience, and competencies.

(7) **Financial information**: The financial affairs of an offender may provide some insight into his or her personality and ability to handle business. Information regarding the debts or spending habits of the offender's *spouse* may also reveal a source of stress in the offender's life and help to explain his or her current difficulties. In such cases, the probation officer must keep in mind that rehabilitation may involve working with the spouse as well as the offender.

(8) **Mental and physical health**: Emotional and physical problems may play an important role in the difficulties of certain offenders. Physical conditions such as epilepsy, brain tumors, diabetes, glandular imbalances, and addiction to drugs or alcohol can cause behavioral disorders. Similarly, psychological problems can be both a source and a result of physical disorders: Obesity, for example, can bring about damaging feelings of inferiority while at the same time being a result of such feelings. Thus, the reporting officer should be aware of—and describe—any physical or psychological condition which may have caused or contributed to the offender's present difficulties.

(9) **Military experience**: Where applicable, the offender's military records may indicate his or her ability to accept and adjust to the regimented structure of military life.

(10) **Evaluation:** This portion of the PSI report should pull together the information in previous sections and present a capsule evaluation of the offender and his or her situation. Any dynamics in this situation should be noted here; and the evaluation may be combined with the reporter's recommendation (below).

(11) **Recommendation:** Except where the court does not want or permit recommendations from the probation officer, the final portion of the PSI report should outline the officer's suggested plan for the convicted offender. Incarceration may be recommended where the officer feels that the offender would be a poor risk for probation and that stronger controls are necessary. In other appropriate situations, the officer may recommend probation, placement in a foster home or residential community treatment center, or both.

f. **General consideration in writing PSI reports:** The value of pre-sentence investigation reports depends on the degree to which they are objective, reliable, and timely.

(1) **Objectivity:** It is generally agreed that in conducting the pre-sentence investigation and writing the PSI report, the probation officer should strive to be objective. At the same time, one must acknowledge the current debate over the general role of the probation officer—that is, whether the officer should simply be a "reporter" or an "advocate" for the interests of the probationer-client or some other party. This issue is discussed in more detail later in the text.

(2) **Verification of facts:** Whenever possible, the reporting officer should obtain verifications for information presented in the report. These can take the form of letters or certified statements; many probation departments have forms that are sent to appropriate agencies in order to secure information about prior arrests, employment, military service, education, medical history, birth, marriage, and divorce.

   Note: Some items of information may be hard to verify—especially where an agency is reluctant to release information that it believes may be confidential. Nevertheless, every effort should be made to verify such information.

(3) **Timeliness:** In order to ensure accurate coverage, the PSI report should be written as soon as possible after the investigation. The probation officer should take notes during interviews and jot down additional material if he or she cannot prepare the report immediately after the interviews. However, the officer should allow adequate time to secure information and write the report—usually ten days to two weeks, unless court deadlines make this impossible.[2]

g. **Example of completed PSI report:** A simulated PSI report is shown in Example 3.1. The format is one frequently used in such reports, and covers most of the topic areas referred to in subsection *e*, above.

h. **The selective pre-sentence investigation report:** Not all cases warrant a complete pre-sentence investigation. Consequently, a shortened form of pre-sentence investigation or PSI report is used by federal probation officers in many instances. This short report—known as a selective PSI report—contains only essential information and excludes all secondary data. By focusing on the essentials, the probation officer and the department

Adult Probation and Parole Services

Region IV

Miami, Florida 33157

NAME: Richard Brown

ADDRESS: 7890 Elm Ave.

LEGAL RESIDENCE: Same

AGE: 38

DATE OF BIRTH: 7/16/42

SEX: Male

RACE: White

CITIZENSHIP: U.S.A.

EDUCATION: High School

MARITAL STATUS: Married

DEPENDENTS: Three (wife and two children)

SOC. SEC. NO.: 123-45-6789

FBI NO.: 123456

DETAINERS: None

DATE: September 12, 1980

DOCKET NO.: 83421

OFFENSE: Possession of cocaine

PENALTY:

PLEA: Guilty, 7/10/80

VERDICT:

CUSTODY: Personal Bond

PROSECUTOR: James Nelson

DEFENSE COUNSEL: Ben Hanson

CODEFENDANTS: William White

DISPOSITION:

DATE:

SENTENCING JUDGE:

OTHER DOCKET NOS.: None

PRESENT OFFENSE:

According to the records of the Miami, Florida, Police Department, the Department received a call from an undercover officer that two men were dealing in cocaine. As a result of receiving this information, officers of the Vice Division on June 18, 1980, followed the defendant, Richard Brown, from his home to the dock area of Miami. The defendant parked his car along Edgewater Avenue in front of Pier 22, and was then seen getting out of his car, using the public telephone located in a booth on Palmetto Ave., and returning to his car. After approximately twenty minutes a car driven by the codefendant, William White, parked immediately behind the car driven by defendant. Defendant got out of his car and went to the car of codefendant. He entered the car of codefendant but stayed in the car for no more than two to three minutes.

Two officers of the Miami Police Department converged on the two parked cars just as defendant was exiting from codefendant's car. Defendant was found to have in his possession what appeared to be a small amount of cocaine. A search of codefendant's car revealed more of what appeared to be cocaine. A routine analysis of the substances indicated that both were cocaine. Both men were taken into custody.

A Miami police officer stated that his department had previous information regarding the operations of these two men. Unconfirmed reports had been received that the cocaine originated from an unknown source who had contacts with Colombian drug smugglers. A small quantity of cocaine was later seized by police officers at a tavern owned and operated by codefendant.

Defendant and codefendant were arraigned on a complaint and warrant on June 18, 1980. Both were released on a personal bond.

PAST OFFENSES:

Date	Offense	Place	Disposition
6/1/60	Petty theft	St. James, Mo.	1 year probation

While in his senior year of high school, defendant and a classmate, both 18, were caught in the act of stealing gasoline from a service station. After filling up a five-gallon gasoline tank, they drove away without paying for the gasoline. The service station attendant recorded the license number on defendant's car, and both youths were arrested the next day. Both pleaded guilty to the offense, and both were given probation at the Willow County Adult Probation Department in St. James, Missouri. Defendant completed his one year of probation.

DEFENDANT'S VERSION OF OFFENSE:

The probation officer interviewed the defendant at his home on July 15, 1980. At that time, defendant told the probation officer that approximately four months prior to his arrest he had met the codefendant, William White, at the tavern operated by White. Defendant became a regular customer of the tavern and developed a casual relationship with codefendant. During the course of their developing relationship, codefendant let it be known that he could obtain cocaine for defendant.

Defendant insisted that he did not know where or from whom codefendant was obtaining cocaine. He stated that he had purchased cocaine from codefendant on at least four previous occasions. Whenever he wanted to purchase cocaine, he would call codefendant and they would arrange a meeting for the purchase.

Defendant expressed regret concerning his use of cocaine. He stated that he was "sort of happy" to be caught before he got too deeply involved in the activity. He expressed anger only at himself and his "stupid behavior."

FAMILY HISTORY:

Defendant was born 7/16/42 at St. James, Missouri, the second of four children born to John and Amy Brown. According to his older sister, he was treated very well by both parents. Throughout his childhood and youth, he was a likeable and well-behaved son, according to his mother. The mother did recall the gas-stealing incident in defendant's youth. Other than that, the mother and older sister could not recall any serious behavior problems displayed by defendant.

Defendant's parents moved from Vermont to Missouri one year before defendant was born. The father worked as a repairman on agricultural machinery. The mother worked in a small clothing store. Upon their retirement, they moved into a mobile home located in the Miami, Florida, area. Defendant lived with his parents in Miami until he married, which was one and a half years after the family moved to Miami. Defendant's parents, his older sister, and a brother currently reside in the Miami area. Another brother remained in Saint James, Missouri, and still lives there. Defendant has a close relationship with his parents, visiting them about once a week and on almost all special occasions. His father is described as being in good health and, although retired from full-time employment, does odd jobs such as yard work. The mother is likewise in apparently good health. Other than baby-sitting her grandchildren, she does no paid work.

Defendant's older sister, Jane Smith, age 40, is married to Tom Smith and currently resides with her husband and two children in Coral Gables. Both she and her husband are employed by the Tropic Air Hotel. Both describe their income as adequate and their lives as "happy and contented." They describe their relationship with defendant as quite close.

Defendant's younger brother, Henry Brown, 37, and his wife, Jeanne Brown, live in Pompano Beach. Henry runs a lucrative seafood restaurant called Henry's Hang-Out. They describe their relationship with defendant as a good one, although they do not often socialize because they are so busy. Jeanne Brown added that she and defendant's wife "do not hit it off very well."

Defendant's youngest brother, Mark Brown, 34, is unmarried and still lives in St. James, Missouri. Defendant described Mark as the "black sheep" of the family. This brother's relationship with other members of the family was described as "distant" by all interviewed.

MARITAL RELATIONSHIP:

On January 5, 1962, defendant married Ellen Williams, then age 19, at the First Baptist Church in St. James, Missouri. The two had known each other and dated off and on for a period of at least three years. This was the first marriage for both. She is currently employed as a waitress at Ethyl's Bake Shoppe (see Employment).

Defendant and his wife have two children: Richard, Jr., 15, and Sam, 9. Both sons live at home with their parents. Both are described as well-behaved, active, and healthy. Both attend school and are described as making adequate grades. Both received certificates for perfect attendance at school for the previous year. Both parents describe their relationships with their sons as close and happy. According to neighbors interviewed by the probation officer, the parents display much interest in the care and control of their boys. All members of the family are well accepted in the neighborhood, according to these same sources.

Defendant's wife stated that in its earlier years their marriage relationship was often "stormy." She related that her husband often came home drunk and threatened to beat her up. Although she stated that she came close to leaving him on several occasions, she always somehow managed to be talked out of it by defendant or his family. She described the more recent years of marriage as "basically good."

However, defendant's wife did say that she was shocked and angered by her husband's present offense and that her initial reaction was "to catch the first plane out of Miami to anywhere." After thinking through the various options, she has decided to stay and try to work out the problem. Her husband has apparently convinced her of his determination to meet the problem head-on and to overcome it.

HOME AND NEIGHBORHOOD:

Defendant and his family live in a five-room stucco house which they purchased in 1978 for $38,000. It is located in a large housing development of similar middle-class Anglo families in the Scenic Village section of Miami. Most of the people in the area are employed in some area of the tourist industry. The Brown family has several close friends in the neighborhood.

This house is the fourth the couple has occupied since they were first married. Defendant states that the various moves were made to improve his family's standard of living.

EDUCATION:

Defendant graduated from Jefferson High School in Saint James, Missouri. According to school records, he graduated with a grade average which was near the middle of his class. The records further indicate that he was rarely absent or tardy. On an I.Q. test administered when he was a freshman, defendant scored very near the middle of the distribution with a 97.

In the fall of 1961, defendant entered Central Missouri State University but left in December before the end of his first semester. Defendant stated to the probation officer that he was "just tired of school" and decided to join the Army. Since January of 1979, defendant has attended the Miami Institute of Technology, where he is studying industrial education. Defendant is not yet sure what he wants to do with this education, "but if it's interesting and pays well, I'll do it." According to the records of the Institute, he is doing good work.

EMPLOYMENT:

July 1965 to February 1970 (4 years, 7 months): Defendant was employed at Wilson's Sundries, 54321 Blue Springs Drive, Miami, as a general handyman for $3.10 per hour. Employment ended when he became sick with a chronic backache.

March 1970 to December 1977 (7 years, 7 months): Defendant was employed as a toolmaker's helper at the Irving Manufacturing Company, Irving Road, Miami, starting at $3.00 per hour. At the time he left this job, he was receiving $4.86 per hour. According to the company supervisor interviewed, defendant was a good employee who left for a higher-paying job.

February 1978 to November 1978 (10 months): For this rather short period of time, defendant was employed as a crib attendant for the Signal Manufacturing Company, 23 Alabama Drive, Miami. Although his starting pay was $5.50 per hour and he was promised a pay raise after one year, defendant quit this job because it was "deadly dull." His employer described his work as adequate.

February 1979 to present (1 year, 8 months): Defendant's most recent job has been as a general machine repairman at South Florida Manufacturing Company, Palmetto Avenue, Miami. He started working there for $5.25 per hour and now makes $6.50 per hour. His supervisor describes his work as adequate and characterizes defendant as hard-working and dependable. The supervisor knows of defendant's present offense.

During his interview with the probation officer, defendant stated that he was very worried about losing his present job. He did tell the probation officer that he was planning to tell his supervisor, "since he would find out anyway." He also stated that if his employer let him continue to work there, he would do his utmost to show his appreciation. He added that by going to school at the Institute, he hoped to increase his earning potential.

Defendant's wife is also employed. Like her sister-in-law, she works as a waitress at a coffee shop located in the Tropic Air Hotel. Although she described the wages as rather low, she stated that she received good tips during the tourist season.

FINANCIAL SITUATION:

Assets: The defendant has the following assets:

An equity of $18,000 in a home purchased 8/5/78 in joint ownership with his wife.

A 1976 Chevelle car, paid in full.

A $10,000 full-life life insurance policy with Shavers Inc. of Atlanta.

A $5,000 term insurance policy with Mid-South Insurance Co. of Tampa.

A $10,000 life insurance policy by the Veterans Administration.

A $3,000 Mariner motor boat, paid in full.

A savings account of $522.34 and a checking account containing approximately $200.00 at the Security State Bank of Miami (both accounts as of 9/11/80).

<u>Financial Obligations</u>: There is a balance of approximately $20,000 owed to the Guarantee Savings and Loan, 231 Wilkins Ave., Miami, for the mortgage on the home. Defendant's monthly payment on the home is currently $237.46. The defendant owes Tri-State Finance Co. the amount of $2,235.00 for a loan to help finance his schooling and to pay other family bills. According to defendant and his wife, they have no other bills. A check with the Credit Bureau indicated that they have a good credit rating.

HEALTH:

<u>Physical</u>: Defendant is 5'10" in height and weighs 185 pounds. He has brown hair and eyes. He has a medium complexion and an average build with no unusual characteristics. He wears glasses when he drives. Otherwise he stated to the parole officer that he has no disabling illnesses or injuries. He describes his health as "excellent." Although he once drank liquor to excess, apparently this is no longer a problem. His last physical examination indicates his health is as good as he says it is.

<u>Mental and Emotional</u>: As stated earlier, defendant had an I.Q. test when he was a freshman in high school and scored near the middle of the distribution (97). In terms of the way he related to the probation officer, it would seem that the score underestimates his intellectual capabilities. He speaks very clearly, expressing both his ideas and his feelings in an articulate manner. The defendant appears to be well-adjusted socially and emotionally. He has many friends where he works and where he lives. He seems to enjoy a good relationship with his wife and sons and other relatives who reside in the Miami area. According to his wife, he no longer drinks and seems to be in good control of his emotions. He expresses an enthusiasm for life and is continuously searching for ways to improve his life and those of his loved ones.

MILITARY SERVICE:

According to the Army Records Center at St. Louis, Missouri, defendant joined the United States Army on 3/3/62 (Serial No. 87-654-321). He was discharged honorably on 4/10/65. With the opportunity to serve his country overseas in West Germany, the defendant viewed his military experience in a very positive manner. He stated that he often regrets not making a career of the Army.

EVALUATIVE SUMMARY:

The defendant, Richard Brown, is a 38-year-old Anglo male who entered a plea of guilty to a charge of being in possession of cocaine. The police investigating the case stated that defendant was not involved in the manufacture or distribution of cocaine. Thus it is believed by the police and by the probation officer that defendant will not be subject to the more severe penalties resulting from drug offense convictions.

Richard Brown was born and spent his childhood and youth in St. James, Missouri. He is the second of four children born to John and Amy Brown. It appears that his early home life was normal and acceptable, as was his performance in school. When his parents retired, he moved with them to their new home in Miami. A short time later, at the age of 20, he married his high school girl friend from St. James, Missouri.

Although defendant and his wife experienced some problems early in their marriage, in recent years their relationship is described as a good one. The couple have two sons, aged 15 and 9. According to defendant, his wife, and various neighbors interviewed, defendant has an excellent relationship with both his sons. Richard seems to be very interested in the welfare of his family. In turn, the other members of his family openly express their affection for defendant. This positive attitude toward defendant is also exhibited by his work associates and neighbors.

Defendant completed high school in St. James, Missouri. According to his school records, his I.Q. and scholastic performance were average. Currently, he is enrolled in industrial education classes at the Miami Institute of Technology. He expressed enthusiasm for his course work and hopes to improve his family's standard of living. He served in the U.S. Army and was honorably discharged. His employment record is essentially a good one. He expressed considerable satisfaction with his present employment, and his employer likewise indicates satisfaction with him.

Defendant is apparently very sorry for his behavior. He expressed much anxiety about the effects of his offense on his wife and sons, his parents, and his job. These individuals seem convinced that the defendant genuinely regrets his actions and desires to make changes in his lifestyle. Defendant is resolved that such difficulties will not happen again.

RECOMMENDATION:

In light of the fact defendant deeply regrets his act and seems determined that the offense will not happen again, and in light of the support he enjoys from his family and employer, the probation officer believes that defendant should be allowed to remain at home but supervised on probation. It might also be appropriate to refer him to a counseling program such as the one at New Visions, which is designed for adults and meets in the evenings.

Respectfully submitted,

Ralph Nelson

Ralph Nelson
Adult Probation Officer

RN:JH
9/12/80

can save considerable time in collecting information, dictating, typing, and reviewing. The selective PSI report has the following components:

(1) Data on offender ("face sheet");

(2) Present offense (official version);

(3) Defendant's version of offense;

(4) Prior record;

(5) Personal history;

(6) Evaluation summary;

(7) Recommendation.[3]

i. **Example of selective PSI report**: Example 3.2 shows a fictitious "short-form" report. The level of detail in this report should be compared with the longer report, Example 3.1.

j. **Presentation of pre-sentence investigation**: Once the probation officer has gathered and assessed the necessary information, he or she upon request supplies the court with a recommendation concerning disposition of the offender. In rare instances, the court may require the investigating officer to defend or substantiate the information contained in the report. Depending on court policy and the circumstances of a particular case, the investigating officer may or may not be required to attend the disposition hearing.

k. **Legal issues concerning pre-sentence investigations**: Two basic legal questions surround the pre-sentence investigation and the PSI report. The first has to do with the timing of the pre-sentence investigation, and the second with disclosure of the information contained in the PSI report.

(1) **Timing of the investigation**: Presumably, a pre-sentence investigation could be begun prior to actual conviction of a criminal defendant. However, the American Bar Association's *Standards Relating to Sentencing Alternatives and Procedures*[4] advances four reasons why such investigations should be made only *after* a determination of guilt:

(a) **Possible invasion of privacy**: The pre-sentence investigation would be an unwarranted invasion of defendant's privacy if he or she is later acquitted. Since the defendant's friends, relatives, and employer must be questioned and embarrassing questions asked, this should not be done unless the person has been convicted of a criminal offense.

(b) **Possible self-incrimination of defendant**: Some information in a pre-sentence investigation must be obtained directly from the defendant. This puts the defendant in a difficult position: the defendant may wish to cooperate with the probation department (in hopes of avoiding a prison sentence if convicted), but this could involve the discussion of sensitive areas before his or her case has been heard in court.

Example 3.2   SELECTIVE PRE-SENTENCE INVESTIGATION

TROIS LACS COUNTY PROBATION DEPARTMENT

Blue Lake, Minnesota

NAME: John Doe

ALIAS NAME(S): Fred Black

ADDRESS: Trois Lacs County Jail

SOCIAL SECURITY NO.: None

AGE: 17

D.O.B.: 3/10/63

SEX: Male

RACE: White

MARITAL STATUS: Single

SPOUSE'S NAME: N/A

LENGTH OF MARRIAGE: N/A

NUMBER OF MARRIAGES: 0

NO. OF DEPENDENTS: 0

EDUCATION: Less Than Four Years

MILITARY: No

DATES: N/A

DATE REFERRED: 8/25/80

DATE INTERVIEWED: 9/1/80

DATE REPORT WRITTEN: 9/4/80

DOCKET NO.: 3564

OFFENSE: Burglary of a private residence,
Forgery and Passing of credit card

CODEFENDANTS: None

PROSECUTOR: George Mean

ATTORNEY: Dan Slick
COURT-APPOINTED: Yes

BOND: No

JAIL: Yes
NO. DAYS: Approx. 45 days

DATE JAILED: July 15, 1980

PRIOR RECORD: Juvenile Record

PENDING CASES: No

STUDENT? No
WHERE: N/A

EMPLOYED? No
WHERE: N/A

EMPLOYABLE SKILL? Yes
WHAT: Auto Mechanic

INCOME: N/A

RESTITUTION:
MONTHLY PAYMENTS: N/A

DATE(S) OF TRIAL: 8/25/80
SENTENCING: 9/12/80

PRESENT OFFENSES:

On August 15, 1980, John Doe was indicted for the felony offenses of burglary of a private residence and forgery and passing of a stolen credit card. On August 25, 1980, John Doe pleaded guilty to these offenses.

On June 20, 1980, Officer D. Jones, #16, was dispatched to 902 Sandlewood Avenue, Blue Lake, Minnesota, in response to a burglary report. Officer Jones contacted the occupant, Mary Anderson, who advised the officer that a person unknown and unseen by her had entered her residence by forcing open a window in the back of her residence. She stated that the following items were missing:

1) One color TV, RCA, valued at $500.00;
2) One electronic calculator, Texas Instruments, valued at $300.00;
3) Mastercard #TUVWXYZ-OO issued through the Blue Lake National Bank.

On July 11, 1980, Officer Jones received information from Jim Brown, Security Officer of the Blue Lake National Bank, that the above-described credit card had been located in Loon River, Minnesota.

Contact was made with the Sheriff's Department of Loon River on July 12, 1980, which advised that a subject who identified himself as Fred Black was being held in custody. The Sheriff stated that along with the Mastercard, the subject also had in his possession a Texas Instruments electronic calculator.

On July 15, 1980, Officer Green proceeded to Loon River, Minnesota, with a warrant for the arrest of John Doe. Officer Green placed the subject under arrest and transported him to the Trois Lacs County Jail.

PAST RECORD:

10/21/74	P.D., Blue Lake	Escape	Released to State Hospital
10/12/75	P.D., Blue Lake	Escape	Released to State Hospital
8/3/76	P.D., Blue Lake	Escape	Released to State Hospital
4/16/77	P.D., Rivertown	Auto Theft Escape	Released to State Hospital
5/2/78	P.D., Birch Hollow	Runaway	Referred to Trois Lacs Juvenile Probation Department

DEFENDANT'S VERSION OF OFFENSE:

During an interview conducted by this officer on 9/1/80, defendant was polite and cooperative but did not demonstrate remorse for his actions, his attention being focused on probation. There was some indication that he realized the seriousness of his acts and some expressed need for outside help to curb his "stealing tendencies." Defendant freely admitted his involvement in the present offense.

PERSONAL HISTORY:

Defendant is a 17-year-old male. He has been in the Trois Lacs County Jail for the present offense since July 15, 1980. According to defendant's own statements as well as the medical records at the Greenshore State Hospital and the Trois Lacs County Juvenile Court, he was born in Allentown, Wisconsin, to Ruth and John Doe, Sr. His parents were divorced three weeks after defendant was born. During the first four years of his life, defendant lived intermittently with his maternal grandparents and his mother and stepfather.

The records also indicate that at age 5 (in 1968) defendant was placed in the True Faith Home for Children in Milliwac, Wisconsin, and remained there until age 8. During this time he attended Channelview School in Milliwac.

Between 1970 and 1971, defendant's mother (the former Ruth Doe and at this time Ruth Johnson) reappeared in his life. Greenshore State Hospital records show that on December 2, 1971, defendant was admitted to the hospital by Mrs. Ruth Johnson on the basis of "uncontrolled behavior."

At the time of his admission to the State Hospital, defendant was given a psychological evaluation resulting in a diagnosis of "Pseudopsychopathic Schizophrenia, Cerebral Dysfunction." Defendant's mother reported that prior to his commitment, his development had been slow and he simply did not show any interest in people. She also reported that the boy had many behavioral problems as a child.

While in the State Hospital, defendant remained mainly in the Children's Psychiatric Ward (CPW). As time elapsed and visits from his family became infrequent, defendant began running away from the hospital and becoming involved in criminal activities.

On June 3, 1977, defendant was released to the custody of Mrs. Joan Smith, who became his legal guardian. It was later explained to this officer that one of Mrs. Smith's daughters had met defendant and introduced him to her mother. Mrs. Smith became interested in defendant's well-being and decided to help him. Defendant was 14 years old at this time.

Defendant's placement with the Smiths did not curb his criminal activity. As indicated by his juvenile arrest record, he began stealing with more frequency and was arrested several times for theft-related offenses. Defendant openly admits that he "has a stealing habit" but claims that he "can lick it, with a little help."

After several referrals to juvenile authorities, defendant was finally committed to the State Training School on February 20, 1978. While there, defendant claims, he learned the trade of auto mechanics. He also encountered problems and escaped custody several times. Defendant remained at the training school for approximately 2½ years.

Defendant has never been employed on a part-time or full-time basis. He appears to be a "loner," having few shared interests with friends or family. He has had no known religious education, beliefs, or affiliation. As previously noted, his education experience is less than four years and he has no military experience. His interests appear to be largely confined to auto mechanics and the assembly of model airplanes.

Defendant thinks that he will be released from jail soon and placed on probation. He has expressed a desire to return to the Smith home, but that is no longer feasible. Defendant has no meaningful relationships with his family, and has not seen his mother or stepfather since June 1977.

EVALUATION:

Defendant's strengths appear to be:
1. He appears to be in good health.
2. He claims to be skilled as an auto mechanic.
3. Because of his youth, defendant does not have any prior arrests or convictions as an adult.

Defendant's weaknesses appear to be:
1. He has a very limited education.
2. It is evident that defendant has lived a very traumatic life. From his birth to the present, defendant has been placed in foster homes and one mental institution. All placements have apparently had adverse results. Defendant seems to have experienced rejection from a very early age.
3. At age 14, defendant was placed under the care and custody of the State Training School, from which he escaped several times.
4. Defendant openly admits that he likes to steal. His juvenile record shows several arrests for theft-related offenses.
5. In 1971, defendant was diagnosed as schizophrenic by Greenshore State Hospital psychologists.
6. Defendant has no employment history.

Defendant's apparent rehabilitation needs:

1. Defendant's rehabilitation can best be implemented in a controlled and structured environment.
2. While incarcerated, defendant should receive a psychological evaluation and psychiatric treatment.
3. While incarcerated, defendant should enroll in a long-range vocational rehabilitation program.
4. While incarcerated, defendant should also receive basic adult education.

RECOMMENDATION:

It is the recommendation of this Department staff that defendant receive a medium sentence at the Minnesota Department of Adult Corrections.

Respectfully submitted,

Ronald Black

Ronald Black
Adult Probation Officer

(c) **Report not admissible in court**: The PSI report is not admissible in court prior to a finding of guilt or innocence, since it could bias the adjudicative process. For the same reason, information from a pre-sentence investigation—if introduced directly or indirectly—could be prejudicial to the defendant and could be difficult to refute.

(d) **Report may not be needed**: Finally, a pre-sentence investigation and PSI report will be unnecessary if the defendant is acquitted. The valuable time otherwise spent in compiling a PSI report before trial should therefore be devoted to convicted offenders or probationers.

(2) **Disclosure of PSI information**: Whether, or to what degree, the information obtained in a pre-sentence investigation (even *after* conviction) should be disclosed to the offender and his or her counsel has long been a difficult problem. Many judges and probation officers oppose disclosure, while defendants and their attorneys generally seek such information.

(a) **Arguments against disclosure**: The principal arguments against disclosure of the information contained in PSI reports stem from the view that such reports are confidential documents, disclosure of the contents of which can have serious repercussions.

1) **Possible disruption of family and work relationships**: Perhaps the best source of information about an offender is his or her family. Yet the release of information supplied by family members during a pre-sentence investigation could impair the offender's family relationships. The same consideration applies to the employer who provides information about an employee. Damage to such vital relationships in the offender's life undermines the goal of effective reintegration into the community; it may also lead families and employers to refuse cooperation (or to be much less forthcoming) in subsequent PSI's.

2) **Possible damage to relationships with other agencies**: Many welfare and law-enforcement agencies have policies of strict confidentiality with respect to information in their files. When they share such information with probation departments, these agencies expect it to be kept confidential and used only for purposes of rehabilitation or supervision. Probation departments therefore face a loss of the respect and confidence of other agencies if confidential information is released—which in turn could eliminate valuable sources of information and seriously diminish the usefulness of the PSI. In short, the exchange of information and professional assistance with other agencies depends on respect for their policies regarding confidentiality.

3) **Threat of possible retaliation**: Third, some defendants have close ties with dangerous associates. If sensitive and incriminating information about these associates developed during a pre-sentence investigation were to be disclosed, retaliation against the defendant or others might result.[5]

(b) **Arguments favoring disclosure**: The chief arguments for disclosing the information in PSI reports to offenders and their attorneys center on fairness, adequate representation, and the contention that information sources do not "dry up" as a result of such disclosure.

1) **Concern for fairness:** Those who support disclosure assert that convicted offenders should have access to material which concerns them and upon which their sentences may be based. That is, in the interests of fairness an offender deserves the opportunity to delete or correct inaccurate, damaging information and to amplify information which he or she believes is incomplete.

2) **Adequate representation by counsel:** Proponents of disclosure likewise argue that the attorney for an offender must have access to information in the PSI report in order to provide adequate representation for his or her client. Among other things, the attorney (who may have greater mobility than the offender) can investigate such information and correct damaging inaccuracies in the report.

3) **No serious risk of "drying up" information sources:** Finally, those favoring disclosure contend that the purported "drying up" of information sources, which some observers advance as a reason for keeping PSI information secret, is largely a myth. These proponents point to the observations of at least one judge that disclosure of PSI information with certain limitations has not curtailed or diminished the quantity and quality of information made available for the PSI report.[6] Proponents also note that disclosure has not resulted in the lengthy adversarial proceedings which opponents had feared might occur.

(c) **Position in Federal Rules of Criminal Procedure:** Rule 32(c)(3) of the Federal Rules of Criminal Procedure takes a "middle-ground" position between complete disclosure on the one hand and complete secrecy on the other. This rule provides that in most instances the defendant and his or her counsel, upon request, may read the pre-sentence investigation report except for recommendations as to sentencing. Where the court feels that certain information in the report (for example, diagnostic opinions) might interfere with rehabilitation if read by the offender, or if it believes that breaching the confidentiality of certain sources could have serious repercussions, it may provide an oral or written summary of such information and allow the offender and his or her attorney an opportunity to comment on it.

(d) **Opinion of National Advisory Commission:** In contrast to the middle-ground position in the Federal Rules, the National Advisory Commission for Standards and Goals for Corrections suggests that pre-sentence reports be made freely available to both prosecution and defense counsel.[7] The commission notes that jurisdictions permitting disclosure have not experienced the adverse consequences that opponents of disclosure have feared. Furthermore, the commission asserts that if such information were presented as evidence at trial, there could be no claim of confidentiality to block its admission.

2. **The Probation Plan:** In addition to compiling, writing, and presenting the PSI report, the probation officer has the responsibility of developing adequate probation plans. With the

exception of violent, sex, or drug offenders, almost 60 percent of all convicted felons are placed on probation, making it the most common sentencing alternative. This fact, coupled with the unique treatment-supervision problems found in probation, requires the informed study of probationer populations and the development of effective programs to meet their needs.

a. **Study of probation offenders:** One of the more productive approaches to effective program planning has been to study the personality characteristics of specific offender groups. With an understanding of the personality constructs on which certain behavior is based, programs may be tailored to the unique strengths and weaknesses exhibited by offenders in a probation setting. A study recently conducted by James Moore and Robert Shearer in this area[8] takes into consideration three areas of personality: manipulative behavior, self-control, and anxiety. Since behavior manifested in these three areas can significantly affect the probation process, the programming guidelines suggested by this study should enhance the effectiveness of probation.

b. **Development of probation plan:** Analysis of the offender population should be followed by the preparation of a probation program. In this respect, the Moore-Shearer study is also instructive. After intensive analysis of more than four hundred probated felons in the state of Texas, the researchers proposed a two-stage probation plan, as follows:

(1) **Stage 1:** According to Moore and Shearer, the initial program for a probated felon should involve a highly structured, written contract in which behavioral objectives, expectations, and consequences are clearly articulated and in which a timetable for assessing progress is incorporated. The probation officer should assume initial control over all decision making, and should assert the power of his position in an even-handed, consistent manner. At the same time, efforts should be made to establish clear, unambiguous lines of communication between the officer and the probationer.

(2) **Stage 2:** Depending on the probationer's behavior, Moore and Shearer envision that the initial probation stage will evolve into a second programming phase. Here, "mutual agreement programming"—in which the probationer assumes a role in decision making and responsibility for the consequences of his decisions—may be implemented. Short-range, intermediate, and long-term goals with clearly articulated (written) reward schedules should be developed; and supervision may be decreased as the probationer assumes an increasing role in his or her rehabilitation program.[9]

NOTES

[1] President's Commission on Law Enforcement and Administration of Justice, *Task Force Report: The Courts* (Washington, D.C.: U.S. Government Printing Office, 1967), p. 18.

[2] Administrative Office of the United States Courts, Division of Probation, *The Presentence Report*, Publication No. 103 (Washington, D.C.: U.S. Government Printing Office, 1965), pp. 1-21.

[3] Administrative Office of the United States Courts, Division of Probation, "The Selective Presentence Investigation Report," *Federal Probation* (December 1974), pp. 47-54.

[4] American Bar Association, *Standards Relating to Sentencing Alternatives and Procedures. Article 4.2 Commentary.* (New York: Institute of Judicial Administration, 1968).

[5] James B. Parsons, "The Presentence Report Must Be Preserved as a Confidential Document," *Federal Probation* (March 1964), pp. 3-7.

[6] Roszel C. Thomsen, "Confidentiality of the Presentence Report: A Middle Position," *Federal Probation* (March 1964), pp. 8-10.

[7] National Advisory Commission on Criminal Justice Standards and Goals, *Corrections* (Washington, D.C.: U.S. Government Printing Office, 1973), pp. 188-89.

[8] Robert Shearer and James Moore, "Personality Dimensions of Felonious Probationers in Texas." Paper presented at the meeting of the American Society of Criminology, Dallas, Texas, November 1978.

[9] *Ibid.*

IV. PAROLE: IN GENERAL

A. BASIC SCOPE AND FUNCTIONS OF PAROLE

1. **Scope of Parole:** The term "parole" is derived from the French and is used in the sense of "*Je donne ma parole d'honneur*"—that is, "I give my word of honor." Ironically, the French themselves prefer the term "conditional liberation" for the phenomenon called "parole" in the United States.[1]

   a. **Parole as a process:** In one sense, parole is a procedure whereby a prison inmate is released prior to the expiration of his or her sentence in order to serve the remaining portion thereof in the community, subject to conditions, supervision, and possible return to prison if the conditions of release are not met. The decision to grant parole, together with the timing and terms thereof, is the responsibility of an agency in the executive branch of government (typically a parole board).

   b. **Parole as a legal status:** A convicted offender on parole is generally considered to be in constructive custody. Thus, parole does not involve a review of or reduction in the sentence originally imposed by the court: It merely affects where, and under what conditions, the sentence may be served. The parolee is not freed, but continues to serve his or her sentence outside the prison and remains subject to the controls or conditions of his or her release.[2]

2. **Distinctive Features of Parole:** Parole can be distinguished from other forms of prison release procedures by its underlying assumptions that the decision to release should be individualized (so as to be optimally timed in the best interests of society and the offender) and that release should be followed by a period of supervision, in order to maximize the chances for a successful reintegration into the community.

   a. **"Individualization" of release decision:** The parole process assumes that the decision to release a prisoner—and the timing of the release—should be based on a thorough knowledge of the offender, an evaluation of his or her incarceration experience, and an adequate assessment of whether community conditions are suitable for his or her release. Statutes establish the boundaries within which the trial judge initially establishes a sentence; but neither the legislature nor the courts can adequately determine beforehand how long each offender should be incarcerated for rehabilitation and for the protection of society. The parole board, with the help of the parole officer, is charged with making this decision.

      Practical limitations on "individualization" approach: If "individualization" of parole is to operate properly, the approach should be to ascertain the point in a prisoner's sentence when he or she is most likely to make an adequate adjustment if returned to society and to time his or her release accordingly. In practice, of course, one cannot predict this precise moment with certainty. Of greater concern is the fact that release decisions may be influenced by factors unrelated to the prisoner's own circumstances. In many states, for example, paroles are deliberately accelerated to relieve overcrowding in prisons—which may undermine the goal of successful reintegration and create problems in protecting society.

b. **Supervision following release**: Supervision of the parolee after release is another major link in the chain of correctional rehabilitation. It is assumed that planning, guidance, and supervision are integral parts of parole, especially during the period immediately following release. Whether or not the parolee successfully reintegrates into the community often hinges on the adjustments made and the degree and type of supervision employed at this critical and difficult time.

3. **Basic Functions of Parole**: Supporters of parole ascribe the following basic functions and advantages to the system as a means of dealing with criminal offenders:

a. **Provides timing of release**: The parole system is designed to time the prisoner's release from prison so that it coincides with the point when he or she is most likely to benefit from release. (Keep in mind, however, that other factors such as prison overcrowding may also influence the timing of release.)

b. **Provides supervision of released prisoners**: The guidance provided by parole supervision offers a partial solution to the problem of readjustment for released prisoners. Unlike the prisoner who is simply turned loose to cope as best he or she can on the outside, a parolee will have a structured adjustment in several important areas of his or her new life on the outside.

c. **More economical than incarceration**: Many studies have verified the common-sense observation that supervising a person on parole is much cheaper than keeping him or her in prison. Not only are the costs of institutionalization avoided, but in many cases the prisoner will be able to work to support his or her dependents—thereby keeping them off the welfare rolls.

d. **Helps avoid the "criminalization" process**: Parole may reduce (or reverse) a "criminalization" process which can otherwise result from a prisoner's exposure to the detrimental effects of a prison environment. These detrimental influences can take several forms: They may be psychological (for example, a lowered self-image or development of a criminal identification); they may be sociological, as when the offender is labeled as and suffers the stigma of being a prisoner; and they may be economic, as when the offender is refused employment because of his or her record as a long-term prisoner. By shortening the time spent in an institution, parole helps to moderate these influences.

e. **Facilitates rehabilitation**: As a corollary effect, the availability of parole offers prison inmates hope and encourages them to make appropriate changes in attitude and behavior so that they may obtain it. Release on parole conveys a vote of confidence in the prisoner's ability to readjust to life in the community; and it also aids rehabilitation by enabling the offender to reassume family and community roles as soon as possible.

f. **Aids prison management and administration**: Among the strongest supporters of parole are prison administrators and staff, who believe that the system gives inmates a positive goal and a compelling reason for cooperating in prison controls and administration.

g. **Helps protect society**: Finally, it is asserted that parole serves an important function in protecting society from criminal behavior. Nearly all prisoners are eventually released from prison; but parole, in contrast to outright discharge, provides for control and supervision following release and thus provides more protection for the community during the period when the risk of recidivism is greatest.

B. HISTORICAL DEVELOPMENT OF PAROLE

The modern-day system of parole has its roots in several earlier developments, the most important of which were the transportation of criminals to colonies in America and Australia, the English and Irish experiences with ticket-of-leave systems, and U.S. prison reforms during the nineteenth century.[3]

1. **Transportation of Offenders to American Colonies:** The transportation of English criminals to the American colonies began in the early nineteenth century, under laws permitting the banishment of criminals who were viewed as dangerous.

   a. **Reasons for transportation:** The English government established the transportation program as a partial solution to difficult economic conditions, in particular the widespread unemployment in England and a labor shortage in the American colonies. The King accepted the granting of reprieves and stays of execution to felons considered physically able to work in the colonies; and the program was supported by the London, Virginia, and Massachusetts Companies and other shipping and trade organizations.

   b. **Conditional pardons:** At first, no specific conditions were placed on the pardons of those convicts who were to be transported. As a result, many evaded transportation altogether or found ways to return to England before their sentences expired. The English government thus found it necessary to impose restrictions on pardons, and to provide for nullification of the pardon if the recipient failed to abide by such conditions. The manner and timing of their return to England were among the principal conditions imposed on the transported criminals.

   c. **Sale of "property in service" rights:** Initially, the English government paid shipping company contractors a fee for each prisoner transported to the colonies. Beginning in 1717, however, the contracting company was given the "property in service" rights of the offender instead of cash; and the government took no further interest in the convict's welfare or behavior unless he violated the conditions of the pardon by returning to England before the end of his sentence. After his arrival in the colonies, the labor or "services" of the prisoner were sold by the shipping company to the highest bidder— that is, the convict became an *indentured servant.*

   The system of indentured servitude dates back to the sixteenth century, and at that time had nothing to do with convicted criminals. The original indenture was used as a means of training novices and providing them with entry into a trade, and involved a written contract specifying the conditions under which an apprentice was indentured to his master. The terms imposed in these contracts of indenture, however, were similar to conditions of parole today.

2. **Transportation of Offenders to Australia:** The Revolutionary War brought an end to the transporting of English criminals to the United States. Prison facilities in England became increasingly overcrowded, which resulted in a more liberal granting of pardons. This in turn was blamed for a serious crime wave in the country; and the public demanded resumption

of a transportation system. Australia was chosen as an appropriate site for convict settlements, the first load of offenders arriving there in 1788.

a. **Differences between Australian and American transportation**: Transportation to Australia differed from transportation to the American colonies in that prisoners in the former system remained under the control of the English government rather than being indentured. The government assumed all transportation and maintenance costs, and the local governor was given "property in service" rights over the convicts. Such rights could then be assigned to free settlers in Australia, who would assume the "property in service" contract.

b. **Introduction of Alexander Maconochie into Australian penal system**: More than any other individual, Alexander Maconochie is credited with being "the father of parole." Born in Scotland, Maconochie was captured by the enemy while serving with the Royal Navy and experienced life as a prisoner at first hand. In a later visit to the new colony of Australia, he was aghast at conditions in the prisons and reported his observations to the English government on his return. Parliament then offered Maconochie a position as superintendent of the Australian prison at Norfolk Island, which he accepted.

c. **Reforms of system under Maconochie**: During his four years at Norfolk Island, Maconochie initiated a number of radical, humanitarian reforms in the Australian penal system. Some of these were primarily symbolic, such as his act of tearing down the prison gallows upon his arrival, his abolition of rules requiring servility by prisoners toward prison staff, and his policy of mingling freely with inmates. Other reforms, however, went to the structure and philosophy of the system itself.

(1) **Modification of legal procedures**: Under Maconochie's administration, prisoners accused of wrongful actions were given court trials open to the public. Prisoners with satisfactory records were selected as jurors for these proceedings; and arbitrary or degrading punishments were forbidden. Chains were used only when deemed necessary for prison security.

(2) **Introduction of humanizing practices**: Maconochie likewise attempted to humanize prison conditions through such practices as distributing books (to encourage reading), allowing prisoners to eat with utensils, and holding funeral services for convicts who died in prison.

(3) **Introduction of "mark system"**: Perhaps the best-known and most important of the reforms instituted by Maconochie was the "mark system," named after the marks that constituted a convict's wages. In the existing system, a prisoner was required to serve a definite sentence; but under the new program he could earn early release through hard work and conformity with prison rules. Convicts were awarded ten marks for a fair day's work, and extra marks were allotted for overtime and for especially hard work. Marks had two uses: They could purchase rations, or they could reduce an inmate's sentence. The mark system gave prisoners new hope of an earlier return to England and served as a valuable incentive for hard work and good behavior.

(4) **Introduction of "graduated release"**: A major goal of Maconochie's mark system was to have inmates accept gradually increasing degrees of social responsibility before

being returned to community life. The system evolved into a five-stage program of "graduated release," as follows:

(a) **Strict custody**: During the first stage of their confinement, convicts worked in prison enclosures under strict discipline.

(b) **Labor in government gangs**: The next stage in prison life was intended to be a socializing period. Labor was divided among six-man work gangs, and prisoners were allowed to choose their workmates.

(c) **Limited freedom**: After prisoners had demonstrated that they could work and live together in groups, they were allowed limited freedoms designed to restore a measure of their individuality and self-respect.

(d) **"Tickets of leave"**: In this next-to-last stage, prisoners who had accumulated sufficient marks were entitled to "tickets of leave" and theoretically could go anywhere, including back to England. (The ticket-of-leave concept is discussed in more detail below.)

(e) **Full freedom**: The last stage in the system of "graduated release" involved the restoration of full and unsupervised liberty to the prisoner.

d. **End of the Maconochie era**: The changes and innovations instituted by Alexander Maconochie were not welcomed by all of his superiors. Maconochie's construction of schools and churches and his designation of a holiday for convicts in honor of the Queen's birthday angered critics. As a result of these and other "radical" reforms, Maconochie was removed from his post in 1844, and conditions at Norfolk Island reverted to their previous state.

e. **Curtailment of prisoner transportation to Australia**: As the number of free English settlers in Australia increased, protests grew over the use of their new homeland as a dumping ground for convicts. The English government, hoping to still these complaints, initiated a so-called Selection System whereby prisoners underwent an eighteen-month training program before being transported to Australia. This system is significant in the development of modern parole, since it marked the first use of trained individuals to evaluate whether prisoners had improved as the result of a training program. (Indeed, the three prison commissioners appointed to make such evaluations are thought to be the forerunners of the three-member parole boards later established by American prison reformers.) However, the Selection System was not successful; and in 1867 the government ended transportation of prisoners to Australia.

3. **Release by "Ticket of Leave"**: The ticket-of-leave system—which involved the release of prisoners on a conditional pardon—was initiated by the English in New South Wales, Australia, in 1790. The local governor was given the right to release prisoners of his choosing on this basis and, at least originally, there was no subsequent governmental supervision of those released. Many such prisoners were given grants of land, and some even had new convicts assigned to work for them!

a. **Penal Servitude Act of 1853**: The Penal Servitude Act passed by Parliament in 1853 gave official, legal status to the ticket-of-leave system in England and Ireland. The act was designed to cut back on transportation of convicts to Australia by substituting a plan of incarceration in English prisons with the possibility of conditional releases on a ticket of leave. Under the plan set forth in the act, offenders with sentences of less than fourteen years were committed to prisons; and where the sentence was greater than fourteen years, judges had the option of ordering transportation to Australia or incarceration. The act also spelled out the length of time in prison required before a convict could receive a ticket of leave.

b. **Problems with system in England:** The ticket-of-leave program in England did not bring about the results anticipated by the public, which mistakenly assumed that prisoners selected for a ticket of leave had demonstrated a favorable response to prison training programs and would be well supervised during the period of conditional pardon following their release. In fact, the ticket-of-leave system was plagued by poor communication and administration, and supervision of those released ranged from the negligible to the nonexistent. An outbreak of serious crime in England further reduced public confidence in the program, and it soon came to be regarded as a failure.

c. **Ireland's experience with tickets of leave:** Ireland enjoyed a more favorable experience with the ticket-of-leave system, owing to the leadership of Sir William Crofton. Crofton was appointed director of the Irish Prison System in 1854, one year after passage of the Penal Servitude Act; and he interpreted the new law as making penal institutions responsible for the reformation of prisoners. So, in his view, tickets of leave would be given only to convicts demonstrating favorable achievements and changes in attitude. The Irish system as subsequently devised and developed by Crofton gained international attention, and had the following basic features:

(1) **Stages of servitude:** From Maconochie's approach in Australia (discussed previously), Crofton borrowed the concept of supervised stages of imprisonment. The Irish system had three stages of penal servitude, including a second stage in which the prisoner's classification was determined by marks awarded for good conduct and for achievement in work and education.

(2) **Indeterminate sentences:** The Irish program also made use of indeterminate (rather than fixed-term) sentences. This made the date of release flexible, and provided an incentive for rehabilitation among prisoners.

(3) **Improved prison conditions:** Crofton believed that the restraints imposed in prisons should not exceed what was necessary to maintain order. Consequently, he sought to make conditions in the prison as nearly like those in the outside world as possible.

(4) **Supervised release:** The ticket-of-leave system in Ireland differed most significantly from the English system in the area of supervision of released prisoners. The Irish ticket of leave required close supervision by the police in all areas except Dublin, where an Inspector of Released Prisoners was given that responsibility. Among other things, supervisors helped the released prisoners secure employment and checked up on their places of residence.

(5) **Confidence in system:** A final and very important characteristic of the Irish system was the degree of support that it enjoyed. In sharp contrast to the English system, the Irish program enjoyed the support of law-enforcement officials, prisoners, and

the general public. Such confidence was both a cause of and a contributor to the overall success of the program.

4. U.S. Prison Reforms During the Nineteenth Century

a. **Groundwork for modern parole system:** The development of the current parole system in the United States can be traced to three important penal reforms that emerged during the nineteenth century: indeterminate sentences, rewards for good conduct, and supervision of persons released on parole.

(1) **Indeterminate sentences:** The success of European prison and correctional programs, especially the Irish system, was not lost on American prison reformers. As the result of prodding by Zebulon Brockway, one of these early reformers, the state of Michigan in 1869 became the first jurisdiction to approve an indeterminate-sentence law. While this particular law was later declared unconstitutional, indeterminate sentences were approved in many states—often in conjunction with the passage of parole laws.

(2) **Rewards for good conduct:** Official recognition of and reward for good conduct on the part of prisoners occurred as early as the New York "good time" law of 1817. Parole has always included the concept of good conduct, in that the agreement for release of a prisoner on parole stipulates that violation of the conditions of his or her release may entail a return to prison.

(3) **Supervision of parolees:** From the beginning, parole in the United States has been based on the notion of supervision. Originally, supervision was accomplished solely by volunteers. In the case of juveniles, the masters of houses of refuge often undertook the responsibility of guardianship and supervision. Adult prisoners were frequently supervised by prison reform societies, such as the Philadelphia Society for Alleviating the Miseries of Public Prisoners. The state of Massachusetts is credited with appointing the first paid supervisor of released prisoners in 1845; and such paid professionals thereafter came to replace volunteer supervisors almost entirely in the United States.

In recent years, volunteers have again become a part of the parole system in this country. Today, however, volunteer supervisors complement rather than replace professionals in providing services to parolees. (The role of volunteers in parole work is discussed more fully in Chapter VIII of the text.)

b. **First American parole system—Elmira Reformatory:** In 1876, a new reformatory was opened at Elmira, New York, with prison reformer Zebulon Brockway as its superintendent. Upon assuming direction of the reformatory, Brockway succeeded in getting an indeterminate-sentence law passed in New York; and the first U.S. parole system emerged from that law. The Elmira parole program had the following basic features:

(1) **Grading system:** Brockway adopted a procedure for grading inmates on their conduct and achievements, following the principles of the mark system originated by Alexander Maconochie in Australia.

(2) **Educational system:** An educational program was compulsory for the young men serving sentences at Elmira.

(3) **Selection for release:** Brockway likewise developed a system for the careful selection of prisoners to be released in this first parole program.

(4) **Volunteer supervision:** Volunteer citizens, referred to as "guardians," were appointed to supervise parolees.

(5) **Short parole periods:** It was believed that parole supervision should not exceed six months; and Elmira followed this policy of short parole periods.

(6) **Reporting:** In order to ensure effective control, a parolee was required to report to his guardian at the first of each month and to submit to the reformatory a written report signed by his guardian and employer.

(7) **Indeterminate sentences:** As noted previously, one of Brockway's first accomplishments at Elmira was to secure the adoption of an indeterminate-sentence law in New York State. Indeterminate sentences were considered a vital part of the correctional concept, since they gave offenders an incentive to change their behavior and attitudes.

c. **Spread of parole and indeterminate-sentence laws:** Following the experience at Elmira, parole systems spread much more rapidly than did the concept of indeterminate sentences. By 1901, for example, twenty states had parole statutes while only eleven had passed indeterminate-sentence laws. This trend has continued up to the present time.

C. ORGANIZATION OF PAROLE SERVICES

1. **Location of Services in Governmental Structure:** Except for a few cases in which juvenile aftercare is a local function, both juvenile and adult parole are administered at the state level. And in all cases, parole is a function of the executive branch of government.[4] This relatively uniform pattern contrasts sharply with the varied organizational arrangements of probation, which may be statewide or localized, in the judicial or executive branch, or any combination of the foregoing. (See discussion in Chapter II.)

2. **Major Components of Parole System:** Parole systems are divided along functional lines between those who are primarily involved in the parole decision-making process and those who administer services to parolees. The decision-making process is the responsibility of a parole board (or other agency with a similar function). The provision of services to parolees in turn can be divided into two components: institutional parole and field parole.

   a. **Institutional parole services:** The major function of the institutional parole staff is investigative; that is, they interview inmates and prepare pre-parole reports to be used in the decision-making process of the parole board. The institutional staff may also help inmates who are about to be released obtain placement in a halfway house or other community-based correctional program.

   (1) Normally, an institutional parole officer interviews all new prison inmates, informing them about the policies and operations of the parole system. Information from these interviews and from other sources (such as psychiatric or psychological reports and pre-sentence reports compiled by probation officers) is used as a guide in developing institutional programs for inmates.

(2) Before consideration for parole takes place, the institutional parole officer again interviews the inmate and compiles the pre-parole report to be used by the parole board in its deliberations. If an inmate receives parole, an officer will meet with him or her to discuss the supervision plan and the conditions of release on parole.

(3) In some cases, the institutional parole staff must notify the law-enforcement agency, prosecutor, or court in the jurisdiction where an inmate was arrested, prosecuted, or convicted when that inmate becomes eligible for parole consideration. And where the inmate is to be released on parole in another state, the staff may be responsible for devising a parole program under the procedures of the Interstate Compact.

b. **Parole boards:** The parole board is the duly constituted agency responsible for deciding whether an inmate should be released on parole or remain in prison. In a limited number of states, the parole board merely makes suggestions on parole to an independent, final decision maker (for example, the governor or state welfare board). In all other states, however, the parole board has sole decision-making power. Parole boards are also responsible for establishing policy and for providing various administrative services; and they are involved in fixing the terms of parole.

(1) **Size of parole boards:** In general, parole boards are composed of three members— although several boards have five members and one has twelve. The total number of parole board members in the United States has increased somewhat in recent years, reaching more than 260 in 1976.[5]

> **Role of hearing officers:** In an effort to ease the workload for the relatively small number of members on a parole board, a number of states have introduced "hearing officers" or "commissioners" into the parole process. While the powers and functions of these hearing officers vary from state to state, they are typically employed in such decision-making processes as parole granting, parole revocation, and work or educational release hearings. Policy making and administrative functions, however, are likely to be reserved for parole board members.

(2) **Full-time or part-time boards:** Some parole board members serve in that capacity on a part-time basis, and have a wide variety of other duties to perform. However, the current trend is to have board members involved only with functions directly related to the parole decision-making process.[6]

(3) **Qualifications of board members:** Historically, there have been few if any established qualifications for parole board members. In recent years, an attempt has been made to provide standards; and by 1976, some thirty-five states had established statutory requirements for board membership. While these requirements tend to be rather vague and general in nature,[7] they do evidence a concern for personality, experience, education, and sex- and minority-group composition in the selection of board members.

(4) **Methods for selection of parole board members:** The most common procedure for selecting parole board members is appointment by the state governor, a method followed in forty of the fifty states as of 1976. In the remaining ten states, board members were appointed by a committee of state officials, by the head of another state department, or by civil service procedures.[8]

(5) **Basic models for parole authorities:** Three basic organizational patterns or models for parole authorities exist in this country. These are referred to as the institutional, independent, and consolidated models; and they differ in their relationships to the general correctional system and in the age level of the offenders whom they serve.[9]

(a) **Institutional model:** This pattern of authority is most common in juvenile parole, and consists of the staff at training schools or correctional institutions where juveniles have been committed. The strongest argument in favor of the institutional model is that those with decision-making power have had direct contact with the clients and are thus most familiar with them and best qualified to determine whether parole is appropriate. Opponents of the method, however, contend that it often places the concerns of the institution (such as economics and internal politics) ahead of the interests of the offender and the protection of society. In addition, they argue that the actual decision-making process tends to be informal and covert, and hence cannot be easily evaluated. Finally, opponents note that adjustment to institutional life—which is likely to be the major criterion for parole in this model—may be a poor indication of the inmate's ability to adjust in the community.

(b) **Independent model:** Under the independent model of authority, parole boards are composed of persons not associated with correctional institutions. This model is intended as an improvement over the institutional pattern of authority and is commonly used today in adult parole systems.

1) Proponents of the independent model assert that parole boards that are independent of correctional institutions will be more aware of and concerned about the general interests of society and the inmates they serve. It is also contended that such boards are likely to be more impersonal and objective in their decision making than those in the institutional authority pattern.

2) Opponents of the independent authority pattern argue that board members in this model are frequently insensitive to the needs of correctional institutions, lack familiarity with the prisoners over whom they have power, and are unduly influenced by political concerns. Moreover, critics contend that the basis for appointment to these independent boards is often little more than political patronage.

(c) **Consolidated model:** The consolidated model is likewise used in adult parole systems, and is intended to embody the advantages (and to minimize the disadvantages) of both the institutional and the independent models. This authority pattern is one result of a trend toward consolidation of field and institutional programs into a single parole department. Although the parole board in this model is part of the state correctional system, board members are not actually on the staff of any particular institution.

1) Those who favor the consolidated model contend that parole boards therein appreciate the programs and needs of correctional institutions but are sufficiently removed from the institutions to permit a broader perspective in decision making. Furthermore, it is argued, board members are more likely to be appointed on the basis of their competence in the field than is the case under the independent model.

2) However, critics of the model assert that consolidated parole boards cannot be truly free of the influence of correctional institutions unless board members are independent of the institutions. Whatever the merits of this argument, the number of consolidated parole board systems has declined in recent years.

(6) **Summary of parole board features in U.S.:** Tables 4.1 and 4.2 provide a summary view of state and federal paroling authorities in this country as of 1976. Table 4.1 lists the organizational structure of the respective boards, while Table 4.2 indicates the basic features of each body.

c. **Field parole services:** The third major component of a parole system is the supervision of, and provision of services to, inmates who have been released into the community on parole. This task is generally assigned to parole officers located in regional offices throughout the state.

(1) **Basic duties of parole officers:** The field service staff is responsible for carrying out the twin objectives of parole—namely, a successful reintegration of parolees into the community and protection of the public during the reintegration process. The duties of parole officers thus include casework counseling and management, coordination of community resources available to parolees, and the application of controls over parolee behavior when this is appropriate or necessary.

(2) **Qualifications of parole officers:** Unlike the rather relaxed requirements for parole board membership in most jurisdictions, persons seeking to be parole officers typically must meet certain qualification standards based on objective criteria. These requirements relate to formal education, personal qualities, and (in some instances) previous experience in corrections or a related area of work.

(a) **Education:** A parole officer generally must have at least a bachelor's degree;[10] and some agencies require a master's degree or some specified number of credits earned toward a graduate degree. While parole agencies usually accept degrees in a wide variety of disciplines, most prefer degrees in criminal justice and social work (or a degree in law, behavioral sciences, or business administration).

(b) **Personal qualities:** Similarly, a parole officer must be able to communicate and work effectively with all types of people, including clients, fellow parole officers, and personnel in other agencies; and he or she must be willing to accept the responsibilities and exercise the authority required by the agency. Most of all, the officer must be committed to understanding, accepting, and helping parolees in roles ranging from simple counseling to the wise exercise of authority.

d. **Interrelationships within the parole system:** The relationships between parole boards and parole service staffs (both institutional and field) vary among different parole systems, but there are two basic approaches. Under one approach, the parole board assumes direct control and is in charge of administering the entire parole system. Under the other, institutional and field parole services are considered part of the larger correctional system and thus are administered by a more comprehensive agency than the parole board. Arguments can be advanced in favor of each of these administrative plans, as follows:

Table 4.1

Characteristics of Adult Paroling Authorities, by Jurisdiction, 1976

Jurisdiction	Agency Within Which Authority Is Located	Administrator of Parole Field Services	Number of Board Members	Full-time Board
Alabama	Autonomous	Parole Board	3	Yes
Alaska	Dept. of Health and Social Services	Division of Corrections	5	No
Arizona	Autonomous	Dept. of Corrections	3	Yes
Arkansas	Autonomous	Dept. of Corrections	5	No
California Adult	Dept. of Corrections	Dept. of Corrections	9	Yes
Colorado	Autonomous	Dept. of Institutions	4	Yes
Connecticut	Dept. of Corrections	Dept. of Corrections	11	No[a]
Delaware	Autonomous	Dept. of Adult Corrections	5	No[a]
District of Columbia	Autonomous	Dept. of Corrections	3	Yes
Florida	Autonomous	Dept. of Offender Rehabilitation	7	Yes
Georgia	Autonomous	Dept. of Offender Rehabilitation	5	Yes
Hawaii	Dept. of Social Services and Housing	Parole Board	5	No
Idaho	Board of Corrections	Board of Corrections	5	No
Illinois	Dept. of Corrections	Dept. of Corrections	10	Yes
Indiana	Dept. of Corrections	Adult Authority	5	Yes
Iowa	Autonomous	Bureau of Community Correctional Services	3	No
Kansas	Autonomous	Parole Board	5	No
Kentucky	Bureau of Corrections	Bureau of Corrections	5	Yes
Louisiana	Dept. of Corrections	Dept. of Corrections	5	Yes
Maine	Autonomous	Bureau of Corrections	5	No
Maryland	Dept. of Public Safety and Correctional Services	Dept. of Public Safety and Correctional Services	7	Yes
Massachusetts	Dept. of Corrections	Parole Board	7	Yes
Michigan	Correctional Dept.	Correctional Dept.	5	Yes
Minnesota	Autonomous	Dept. of Corrections	5	Yes
Mississippi	Autonomous	Parole Board	5	No[a]
Missouri	Dept. of Special Services	Parole Board	3	Yes
Montana	Dept. of Institutions	Dept. of Institutions	3	No
Nebraska	Board of Pardons	Dept. of Correctional Services	5	No[b]
Nevada	Autonomous	Parole Board	5	No
New Hampshire	Autonomous	Parole Board	3	No
New Jersey	Dept. of Institutions and Agencies	Division of Corrections and Parole	3	Yes
New Mexico	Autonomous	Dept. of Corrections	3	Yes
New York	Dept. of Correctional Services	Dept. of Correctional Services	12	Yes
North Carolina	Dept. of Corrections	Parole Commission	5	Yes
North Dakota	Autonomous	Board of Pardons	3	No
Ohio	Dept. of Rehabilitation and Correction	Adult Parole Authority	7	Yes
Oklahoma	Dept. of Corrections	Dept. of Corrections	5	No
Oregon	Autonomous	Correctional Division	5	Yes
Pennsylvania	Autonomous	Parole Board	5	Yes
Rhode Island	Dept. of Corrections	Dept. of Corrections	5	No
South Carolina	Autonomous	Parole Board	7	No
South Dakota	Autonomous	Division of Corrections	3	No
Tennessee	Dept. of Corrections	Dept. of Corrections	3	Yes
Texas	Autonomous	Parole Board	3	Yes
Utah	Dept. of Corrections	Dept. of Corrections	3	No
Vermont	Autonomous	Dept. of Corrections	5	No
Virginia	Dept. of Corrections	Dept. of Corrections	5	Yes
Washington	Autonomous	Dept. of Social and Health Services	7	Yes
West Virginia	Autonomous	Dept. of Institutions	3	Yes
Wisconsin	Dept. of Health and Social Services	Dept. of Health and Social Services	11	Yes
Wyoming	Autonomous	Parole Board and Governor	3	No
U.S. Parole Commission	Dept. of Justice	Federal District Courts	9	Yes

[a]The chairman serves full-time; members serve part-time.
[b]The chairman and two members serve full-time; two members serve part-time.

Source: Vincent O'Leary and Kathleen J. Hanrahan, *Parole Systems in the United States: A Detailed Description of Their Structure and Procedures,* 3rd ed. (Hackensack, N.J.: National Council on Crime and Delinquency, 1977), pp. 13–15.

Table 4.2

Appointment Procedure, Statutory Qualifications for Membership, and Length of Term for Members of Paroling Authorities, by Jurisdiction, 1976

Jurisdiction	Member Appointed by	Statutory Qualifications for Membership	Length of Term (Years)
Alabama	Governor	None	6
Alaska	Governor	Chairman only: training or experience in field of probation and parole.	4
Arizona	Governor	Broad professional or educational experience with an interest in corrections.	3
Arkansas	Governor	None	5
California Adult	Governor	Broad background in the appraisal of law offenders and the circumstances which bring them to prison.	4
Colorado	Governor	Knowledge of parole, rehabilitation and kindred subjects.	6
Connecticut	Governor	Shall be qualified by training and experience for the consideration of matters before them.	4
Delaware	Governor	Chairman: graduate degree in social work, sociology, psychology, criminology or corrections, and 5 years experience in corrections. Member: demonstrated interest in corrections, treatment or social welfare. One member must be an attorney and one must be a psychologist or psychiatrist.	4
District of Columbia	Mayor of District of Columbia	Knowledge or experience in the field of corrections, law or behavioral science.	6
Florida	Governor	Knowledge of penology and social welfare	6
Georgia	Governor	None	7
Hawaii	Governor	None	4
Idaho	Board of Correction	One must have experience and qualifications in business administration; one must have experience as a peace officer or trained penologist; one must have training and experience as a psychiatrist.	5
Illinois	Governor	Five years experience in penology, corrections, law enforcement, sociology, law, education, social work or medicine. Two of the 3 panel members who hear juvenile cases must have 3 years' experience in juvenile corrections.	Mixed[a]
Indiana	Governor	Prepared by "knowledge, training, and experience" to perform their duties.	4
Iowa	Governor	One member must be a practicing attorney.	6
Kansas	Governor	One member must be a practicing attorney; two members must be drawn from the fields of psychiatry, psychology, sociology or medicine.	4
Kentucky	Governor	Members must demonstrate a knowledge of and experience in correctional treatment or crime prevention.	5
Louisiana	Governor	None	6
Maine	Governor	Special training or experience in law, sociology, psychology or related branches of the social sciences.	4
Maryland	Secretary of Public Safety and Corrections Services	Training or experience in law, sociology, psychology, education, criminology or social services.	6
Massachusetts	Governor	B.A. plus 5 years' experience in parole, psychology, law, sociology, or a related field. Must try to include a psychiatrist, attorney, psychologist and a member of parole staff.	5
Michigan	Civil Service	Career service in corrections; civil service examination.	Life
Minnesota	Governor	Knowledge or experience in corrections or related fields; sound judgment and the ability to consider both the needs of the offender and the safety of the public. Members must include one woman, one man and one member of a racial minority.	6
Mississippi	Governor	Persons who by knowledge and experience are prepared to perform effectively the duties of the Board.	4

Table 4.2 (cont.)

Jurisdiction	Member Appointed by	Statutory Qualifications for Membership	Length of Term (Years)
Missouri	Director of the Department of Social Services	Recognized integrity and honor, known to possess ability, experience and other qualifications fitting them to the position.	6
Montana	Governor	Academic training or experience in criminology, psychiatry, law, education, social work or related fields. At least one member must have particular knowledge of Indian culture and problems.	4
Nebraska	Governor	Good character and judicious temperament. At least one member must be of a minority race, and one member must have professional experience in corrections.	6
Nevada	Governor	None	4
New Hampshire	Governor	None	5
New Jersey	Governor	Of recognized ability in the field of penology, with special training or experience in law, sociology, psychology or related social science fields.	6
New Mexico	Governor	None	3
New York	Governor	None	6
North Carolina	Governor	Recognized ability, training, experience and character.	4
North Dakota	Governor	One member must be a licensed attorney, one experienced in law enforcement and one qualified by education and experience in the field of criminology or behavioral science.	3
Ohio	Civil Service	Required to have education and experience in corrections, law or social work.	Life
Oklahoma	Mixed[b]	None	Coterminous with governor
Oregon	Governor	Competent persons. At least one member must be a woman.	4
Pennsylvania	Governor	Good moral character.	6
Rhode Island	Governor	One: a physician qualified in psychiatry or neurology; one: an attorney; one: a professional trained in corrections or related social work fields. Two members must show an interest in social and welfare problems.	5
South Carolina	Governor	None	6
South Dakota	Mixed[c]	None	4
Tennessee	Governor	Experience or education in the criminal justice system.	6
Texas	Mixed[d]	Good character.	6
Utah	Board of Corrections	None	6
Vermont	Governor	Knowledge and experience in correctional treatment, crime prevention or related fields.	6
Virginia	Governor	None	4
Washington	Governor	None	5
West Virginia	Governor	Experience in the field of social sciences or the administration of penal institutions and familiarity with the principles and practice of those fields.	Pleasure of the governor
Wisconsin	Civil Service	Master's degree in social work, sociology, psychology, correctional administration, or a related field or a degree in law; and six years of progressively responsible relevant work or upper level consultative responsibility either in social service programs or in programs primarily oriented to the needs or problems of adults or juvenile offenders. An equivalent combination of training and experience may be considered.	Life
Wyoming	Governor	None	6
U.S. Parole Commission	President	None	6

[a]Members serve terms of either 2, 4, or 6 years.

[b]Three members are appointed by the governor, one by the presiding judge of the Court of Criminal Appeals, and one by the chief justice of the State Supreme Court.

[c]One member is appointed by the governor; one by the State Supreme Court and the attorney general appoints the assistant attorney general to the board.

[d]One member is appointed by each of the following: the governor, the chief justice of the Supreme Court and the presiding justice of the Court of Criminal Appeals.

Source: Vincent O'Leary and Kathleen J. Hanrahan, *Parole Systems in the United States: A Detailed Description of Their Structure and Procedures*, 3rd ed. (Hackensack, N.J.: National Council on Crime and Delinquency, 1977), pp. 21–24.

(1) **Advantages of control by parole board**

    (a) **Accountability:** The parole board is often held accountable for failures in the parole system, and thus should be able to supervise the entire system.

    (b) **Flexibility:** If the parole board has control over the administration of parole services, it is argued that it can more easily evaluate and make necessary changes in the provision of those services.

    (c) **Advocacy:** Finally, the parole board is alleged to be in the best position to promote the interests of the entire parole system and to generate public support therefor. In other words, parole is less likely to become a mere "stepchild" of the larger correctional system when it is a separate entity administered by the parole board.

(2) **Advantages of control by correctional agency**

    (a) **Continuity:** Admittedly, parole is one part of the larger correctional process; and consistency in philosophy and programs thus may be more readily obtained if it is administered as one segment of corrections. Inter-agency rivalries within the corrections process are theoretically less likely under such an integrated system. Furthermore, the growing number of programs which overlap correctional institutions and parole—work release, educational release, and the like—are probably best administered by a single, centralized agency.

    (b) **Administrative superiority:** It is also argued that parole boards are (or should be) primarily concerned with the decision-making process rather than the day-to-day operations involved in parole supervision or the administration of parole departments. These latter tasks, it is contended, call for different skills and are best supervised by an agency specifically designed for administration of correctional departments and services.

(3) **Current trend toward control by correctional departments:** In recent years, the trend has been toward administration of parole services by correctional agencies, with parole boards concentrating on the decision-making function. Table 4.3 illustrates this shift in the locus of responsibility for field parole services.

Table 4.3

**Administration of Parole Field Services
Adult Paroling Authorities, 1966, 1972, and 1976**

Administrative Parole Field Services	Number of Jurisdictions		
	1966	1972	1976
Paroling authority	31	18	13
Other agency	21	34	39
TOTAL	52	52	52

Source: Vincent O'Leary and Kathleen J. Hanrahan, *Parole Systems in the United States: A Detailed Description of Their Structure and Procedures*, 3rd ed. (Hackensack, N.J.: National Council on Crime and Delinquency, 1977), p. 10.

NOTES

[1] U.S. Department of Justice, *Attorney General's Survey of Release Procedures*, Volume IX: *Parole* (Washington, D.C.: Department of Justice, 1939), pp. 4-5.

[2] *Vernon's Annotated Texas Code of Criminal Procedures*, Article 42.12, 2 (c). (Kansas City, Mo.: Vernon Law Book Co., 1966).

[3] Frederich A. Moran, "The Origins of Parole," *National Probation Association Yearbook* (1945), pp. 71-75.

[4] American Correctional Association, *Directory of Juvenile and Adult Correctional Departments, Institutions, Agencies and Paroling Authorities* (College Park, Md.: American Correctional Association, 1976), pp. 250-57.

[5] Vincent O'Leary and Kathleen J. Hanrahan, *Parole Systems in the United States: A Detailed Description of Their Structures and Procedures*, 3rd ed. (Hackensack, N.J.: National Council on Crime and Delinquency, 1977), pp. 12-15.

[6] *Ibid.*, p. 11.

[7] *Ibid.*, pp. 21-24.

[8] *Ibid.*

[9] National Advisory Commission on Criminal Justice Standards and Goals, *Corrections* (Washington, D.C.: U S. Government Printing Office, 1973), pp. 395-97.

[10] National Planning Association, *A Nationwide Survey of Law Enforcement Criminal Justice Personnel Needs and Resources, Interim Report* (Washington, D.C.: National Planning Association, 1976), pp. v-158.

V. THE DECISION-MAKING PROCESS IN PAROLE

A. EXTENT TO WHICH PAROLE IS USED

Nearly all inmates incarcerated in state and federal prisons are eventually released into the community. While some are released on completion of their sentences, about two-thirds are released by means of parole.[1] Table 5.1 shows the number of adult and juvenile parolees under supervision in 1975, by jurisdiction.

B. IMPACT OF SENTENCING STATUTES ON PAROLE

1. **Varying Impact Under Present Laws:** Parole is the chief means of releasing inmates from prison where sentencing statutes provide long maximum terms that cannot be modified by trial judges, where "good time" laws do not exist, or where pardons are seldom used. Parole is less common in states which require that minimum sentences be served; and a few states have abolished the procedure entirely.

2. **Proposed Sentencing Guidelines:** The National Advisory Commission on Criminal Justice Standards and Goals has suggested a sentencing system that it feels is both practical and consistent with parole objectives. The guidelines—which attempt to strike a balance between judicial and legislative authority, on the one hand, and adequate discretion for the parole agency, on the other—are as follows:

   a. **Maximum limits:** The legislature should establish maximum sentence limits, with the sentencing judge in each case having discretion to fix a sentence within the statutory limit.

   b. **No minimum sentences:** At the same time, neither the legislature nor the courts should impose minimum sentences.

   c. **Short sentences preferred:** For most offenses, the statutory maximum sentence should not exceed five years.

   d. **Mandatory release:** A program of mandatory release with supervision should be established for offenders ineligible for parole, so that such inmates are not held in an institution until their absolute discharge date.

   e. **Parole conditions established by parole agency:** The conditions of parole for offenders should be set by the paroling authority, with the sentencing judge given an opportunity to suggest special conditions.

   f. **Elimination of consecutive sentences:** The legislature should prohibit the accumulation of consecutive sentences by an offender where this would interfere with minimum parole eligibility.

   g. **Alternatives for recidivists:** Legislatures also should provide alternatives to reimprisonment for released prisoners whose paroles are revoked.

Table 5.1

Number of Adult Parole and Juvenile Parole/Aftercare Clients Under State and Local Supervision During 1975, by Sex and by State

| State | Number of Parole/Aftercare Clients Under Supervision During 1975 | | | | | |
| | Adult Parole | | | Juvenile Parole/Aftercare | | |
	Total	Male	Female	Total	Male	Female
TOTAL STATE AND LOCAL	234,096	209,826	24,270	94,140	74,752	19,388
Alabama	4,350	3,985	365	747	565	182
Alaska	214	202	12	(1)	–	–
Arizona	1,236	1,179	57	567	538	29
Arkansas	4,356	4,049	307	1,263	912	351
California	28,322	26,607	1,715	9,573	8,243	1,330
Colorado	2,998	2,804	194	892	713	179
Connecticut	2,752	2,477	275	1,042	726	316
Delaware	416	366	50	381	300	81
District of Columbia	3,628	3,569	59	1,116	893	223
Florida	6,401	5,748	653	6,656	5,343	1,313
Georgia	4,379	3,973	406	3,797	3,007	790
Hawaii	534	524	10	96	64	32
Idaho	493	479	14	336	265	71
Illinois	20,868	12,719	8,149	1,886	1,602	284
Indiana	2,153	2,052	101	1,702	1,392	310
Iowa	780	684	96	1,106	786	320
Kansas	1,865	1,731	134	120	91	29
Kentucky	2,831	2,607	224	2,117	1,612	505
Louisiana	2,384	2,230	154	2,598	2,089	509
Maine	997	900	97	7	5	2
Maryland	8,044	7,641	403	1,174	1,067	107
Massachusetts	3,957	3,742	215	5,887	4,839	1,048
Michigan	7,074	6,672	402	4,969	3,816	1,153
Minnesota	2,309	2,123	186	1,270	1,008	262
Mississippi	1,103	855	248	1,169	1,011	158
Missouri	4,644	3,630	1,014	1,647	1,319	328
Montana	506	460	46	1,028	598	430
Nebraska	1,076	1,010	66	864	626	238
Nevada	382	323	59	810	430	380
New Hampshire	303	294	9	313	283	30
New Jersey	11,066	10,525	541	1,411	1,328	83
New Mexico	3,417	3,158	259	1,223	910	313
New York	17,823	17,181	642	7,280	5,458	1,822
North Carolina	6,793	5,909	884	1,812	1,319	493
North Dakota	170	167	3	39	33	6
Ohio	11,004	9,757	1,247	6,907	5,778	1,129
Oklahoma	3,368	2,863	505	2,797	1,854	943
Oregon	2,145	1,836	309	1,682	1,265	417
Pennsylvania	21,917	20,659	1,258	(1)	–	–
Rhode Island	430	365	65	304	283	21
South Carolina	4,672	4,310	362	1,362	987	375
South Dakota	187	171	16	828	574	254
Tennessee	2,745	2,458	287	3,181	2,506	675
Texas	11,162	10,477	685	2,809	2,391	418
Utah	917	844	73	130	109	21
Vermont	603	535	68	146	134	12
Virginia	4,076	3,743	333	2,230	1,682	548
Washington	5,783	5,058	725	2,931	2,312	619
West Virginia	818	734	84	403	359	44
Wisconsin	3,574	3,380	194	1,323	1,159	164
Wyoming	71	61	10	209	168	41

–Represents zero.

(1)In Alaska and Pennsylvania upon release from institutions, juveniles are placed on probation, not parole or aftercare.

Source: U. S. Department of Justice, Law Enforcement Assistance Administration, State and Local Probation and Parole Systems, No. SD-P-1 (Washington, D.C.: U.S. Government Printing Office, 1978), p. 39

h. **No offenses automatically ineligible for parole**: Finally, there should be no offense for which parole is automatically denied by statute.[2]

C. PREPARATION OF INMATES FOR PAROLE

1. **Underlying Problems**

   a. **Stresses imposed by incarceration**: An offender sentenced to prison undergoes a series of stressful experiences, all of which must be taken into account in preparing him or her for parole. After the reduction in self-esteem resulting from arrest, trial, and sentencing in a public forum, the offender encounters a similar reduction in social status on entering prison. He or she is in a strange, threatening environment, stripped of personal possessions, given anonymous new clothing, and thrust into a community largely devoid of human affection and tenderness.

   b. **Distortions of inmate "counterculture"**: Every prison population has its own "code of ethics" developed from the criminal backgrounds of the inmates. This code establishes many aspects of life in the prison, and generally induces a faulty relationship with authority structures. Inmates are quick to express hostility toward prisoners who do not accept this established culture, so that those who disagree are nonetheless generally forced to accede to it out of fear. Participation in the prison culture in turn isolates an offender from the prison staff; and the offender comes to believe that such authority is something to be avoided, evaded, or manipulated.

   c. **Need for improved self-image**: The stresses of prison life and the distortions imposed by inmate "countercultures" often lead to a loss of self-respect and lowered self-image on the part of the prisoner. The goal, then, must be to change this pattern and restore proper values and perspective. The inmate will need to overcome antisocial habits and develop goals and behavior acceptable in the outside world. This in turn requires training and treatment to convince the prisoner that he or she is not just a "number" but an individual with worth and potential in the community.

2. **Guidelines for Planning Release**: In light of the problems just discussed, the following steps should be observed in preparing inmates for eventual release on parole:

   a. **Begin preparation early**: Preparation of an inmate for release should begin as soon as he or she is admitted to prison. This will help to alleviate anxieties about length of stay, which are particularly acute where the inmate has just begun serving a long sentence.

   b. **Help maintain ties with outside world**: It is important that the inmate keep any positive personal ties that existed prior to imprisonment. He or she should be encouraged to maintain relationships with family, friends, and former employer or business associates; and these relatives and associates likewise should be encouraged to keep in contact with the prisoner through regular visits or correspondence. Similarly, the inmate should be encouraged to keep up with developments in the outside world through magazines, books, and television. This will help to ensure that the inmate does not fall completely out of step with or become overwhelmed by changes in society upon release from prison.

   c. **Develop employment skills**: It is important that the prisoner have legitimate, marketable skills when he or she reenters the community. Thus, part of the preparation for release on parole might include placing the prisoner in a type of employment to which he or she is accustomed or in a trade that he or she might follow after release (for example, prison bakery, machine shop, newspaper).

d. **Arrange suitable post-release employment:** In addition to helping the inmate acquire or retain an employment skill, it is essential to arrange an acceptable job for him or her after release. Ideally, the job should be sufficiently challenging and interesting to generate the prisoner's enthusiasm, 'yet stable enough that he or she will not be easily discouraged by it.

e. **Establish proper attitudes toward release:** Another important factor in preparing inmates for release is the development of proper attitudes concerning release and roles in the outside world. Too often, prisoners are concerned merely with "getting by" rather than with readjusting themselves; and prison staffs may contribute to a defeatist attitude by informing inmates that they are "losers" or that the prison expects to see them again after their release. Efforts therefore must be made to help the prisoner develop a healthy self-image and a positive attitude toward release and life in the community.

3. **Role of Inmate Classification in Preparation Process:** Classification is an important part of the overall treatment of offenders, and thereby influences the preparation of inmates for parole. While differences in personality and in the social situations that have conditioned prisoners make it difficult to classify offenders beyond age, type of offense, and apparent degree of security risk, such attempts should be made; and there should be periodic reevaluations and reclassification of offenders during their progress through the prison program. The basic role of classification in the pre-release period is as follows:

a. **Coordination of services:** Classification helps to direct all prison programs toward release into the community, and thus serves to coordinate the efforts of parole authorities and the prison staff.

b. **Development of individualized treatment programs:** Professional classification systems also make it possible to develop individualized treatment programs for inmates. These have great advantages over unrelated, haphazard services by staff members, especially in the case of sexual psychopaths, alcoholics, drug addicts, mental incompetents, and other offenders with unusual physical or psychological problems.

c. **Use in parole decision making:** In many instances, the prison classification committee and the parole board will meet to discuss inmates who are being considered for parole. The classification committee can supply information on each inmate's adjustment to prison life and any perceived improvement or deterioration in attitude, thereby giving the parole board another basis for deciding whether to grant or refuse parole.[3]

D. THE PAROLE HEARING

A parole hearing is conducted by one or more members of the paroling authority to consider whether an inmate should be released on parole. The hearing thus becomes the focal point of parole decision making.

1. **Variations in Hearing Procedures:** The procedures used in parole hearings vary among jurisdictions throughout the nation.

    a. **Screening of cases for hearing:** In four states, hearings are granted to inmates only after a preliminary review of their cases by a parole staff or parole board member and a determination that they might merit parole. Other states do not use a screening procedure, and a prisoner automatically comes up for parole consideration when he or she has met certain eligibility requirements (whether or not he or she is likely to be granted a release).

    b. **Number of board members participating in hearing:** Jurisdictions also differ in the number of parole board members who attend the parole hearing. In some states, all members of the parole board meet with the inmate in question. In others, however, some lesser number actually attend the parole hearing.

        (1) **Hearings before full parole board:** In twenty-three states, the full parole board hears the case of each person being considered for parole. Since many jurisdictions conduct forty or more hearings in a single day, however, their value in the decision-making process is questionable.

        (2) **Hearings by "working committee" of board members:** In states with several prisons the parole board may be divided into working committees, each of which is authorized to conduct hearings and grant or deny parole. Under this system, a case usually is not referred to the full board unless the panel cannot reach a decision or feels that the matter is too controversial to be decided by only a portion of the board.

        (3) **Hearings by one board member:** In the federal parole system (and in some states), a single parole board member examines the institutional records and interviews the inmate being considered for parole. The member then makes a recommendation for or against parole, which the full board later ratifies or modifies when it meets in executive session.[4]

2. **Inmate Participation at Parole Hearings:** Parole hearings are considerably more effective as a basis for decision making when the inmate is present and allowed to participate.

    a. **Provides sense of individuality:** Participation of inmates at their parole hearings helps to demonstrate that they are being considered as individuals on a case-by-case basis, and that the paroling authority is interested in *their* version of the facts. The reverse is likely to be true where offenders perceive that release decisions are being based on written records or files about which they know little or nothing.

    b. **Hearings improve evaluations:** Even more importantly, inmate participation gives the decision maker the benefit of observing the parole candidate at first hand. In some cases, inmates may reveal themselves to be so different from the picture painted in the written records that board members will reevaluate their feelings about that prisoner's release prospects. This could result in an earlier parole in certain instances and a longer period of incarceration in others.

3. **Informing Inmates of Parole Decisions:** In the past, it was common practice for the inmate

to receive word of the decision on his or her parole from the prison staff several days after the parole hearing. Today, however, twenty-three jurisdictions require that the inmate be informed of the decision by the board immediately after the hearing.[5] This procedure has the following advantages, among others:

a. **Improves evaluation:** The requirement that the board communicate its decision personally to the inmate has the effect of forcing parole board members to evaluate more carefully the reasons for their decisions, since they must be able to explain the decision to the inmate.

b. **Improves communication of decision:** When the individuals who make the decision concerning parole also inform the offender of the decision, any vagueness or error that may result when a third-party staff member undertakes this communication is eliminated.

c. **Clarifies criteria for parole:** Where parole has been denied, discussing the reasons for the decision should give the inmate a better understanding of what is expected of him or her in order to receive parole.

d. **Emphasizes fairness and openness of decision-making process:** Discussing the board's decision with the inmate at the conclusion of the parole hearing fosters a sense of fairness and openness, and helps to counteract any notion that parole decisions are arbitrary or punitive.

e. **Facilitates prison management:** Finally, allowing inmates an opportunity to "ventilate" their views and feelings tends to relieve suppressed hostilities and thus helps in the task of managing the institution.

E. FACTORS IN GRANTING OR DENYING PAROLE

Much depends on the ability of the parole board to grant or refuse parole wisely. A decision to grant parole based on insufficient information or faulty predictions of future behavior can result in subsequent crimes harming society, which serves to discredit the entire parole system. Conversely, failure to release an offender on parole when such release would be beneficial and timely can undermine the correctional process and result in serious injustice to the offender. Hence, the criteria and the data base relied on in making parole decisions are extremely important.

1. **Criteria in Parole Decision Making:** The criteria used by parole boards in reaching their decisions are not usually expressly stated; and such criteria vary somewhat among jurisdictions. However, the following appear to be the factors most widely relied on in the decision-making process:

a. **Probability of recidivism:** Of all criteria considered by parole boards, the likelihood that the inmate will recidivate (that is, commit another criminal offense after release) is the most significant. Parole board members feel responsible for their decisions, not least because they will come under fire if the parolee commits a serious offense.

(1) **Type of offense:** The offense for which the inmate was imprisoned may influence the board's concern for recidivism as a factor in granting or denying parole. In some

cases a low probability of recidivism may be required, while in others the board may grant parole despite a high probability of recidivism.

The *seriousness* of the possible recidivist crime may be the determining factor here. For example, an inmate convicted of a violent crime (such as attempted murder) may be denied parole on the basis of a "medium" probability of recidivism, while one convicted of a nonviolent offense (such as forgery) might be released despite a higher probability of recidivism. This reflects a general public concern for protection from violence.[6]

(2) **Past criminal record**: The inmate's criminal record is likewise relevant in assessing his or her chances of abstaining from criminal activity if released on parole. An inmate with a long criminal record would be considered a greater risk than an inmate with little or no prior record—although this judgment may be modified where the prior offenses were situational and the environment has since changed.

(3) **Changes in personality**: The parole board will look for any change in the inmate's attitudes toward himself or herself and toward his or her past behavior in determining the possibility of recidivism. The assumption is that the prior offense resulted from some personal problem, and that unless gains have been made by the prisoner in solving the problem, future criminal activity is likely to occur.

(4) **Changes in precipitating social situations**: Elements in the prisoner's life situation that directly or indirectly influenced his or her previous criminal behavior are also an indication of possible recidivism. Hence, the parole board will weigh the implications of changes (or lack of same) in such factors as home life or financial situation in analyzing the inmate's chances for a successful parole.

(5) **Adjustment to penal institution**: The inmate's ability to adjust to institutional rules and his or her ability to get along with other inmates and the prison staff is viewed by some parole boards as an indication of the prisoner's ability to adjust to the outside world if released on parole. Thus, participation in the various rehabilitative programs offered at the prison may be considered evidence of a low probability of recidivism even where little other change in the prisoner's personality or attitudes has been observed. By the same token, failure or refusal to participate in institutional programs will probably count against the inmate in the parole board's assessment of the likelihood of recidivism.

(6) **Previous supervision experience**: Many inmates considered for parole have had prior supervision on probation or parole release, and some may even be serving their current sentence as a result of violating the terms of their probation or parole. An inmate's experience under prior supervision may therefore be a good indication of the behavior to be expected if he or she is paroled.

(7) **Adequacy of parole plan**: Finally, proposed plans for employment and residence arrangements may be important factors in assessing the probability of a successful parole for some offenders. Preparation of a good parole plan is a favorable sign, because it indicates that the inmate is thinking about the future. In contrast, a plan deemed inadequate by the parole board may result in denial or delay of parole for that inmate.[7]

b. **Concerns of criminal justice system**: A 1965 National Parole Institute questionnaire revealed that, in addition to probability of recidivism, parole board members considered the following broader social criteria in their decision-making process:

(1) **Equitable treatment**: Much emphasis has been placed on due process in the granting or denial of parole, and on fair treatment generally in all aspects of the parole process.

(2) **Impact of decision on criminal justice system**: The impact of the parole decision on other components of the criminal justice system is likewise a consideration. How parole board policies and actions affect law enforcement, correctional agencies, and the judicial process are all matters of concern to the paroling authority.

(3) **Impact of decision on general public**: The reaction of persons outside the correctional system to particular parole decisions may also be weighed, since parole boards typically are sensitive to public criticism.[8]

c. **Desirability of supervised release**: Parole boards release an inmate on parole near the expiration of his or her sentence when they believe that a period of supervision is preferable to discharging the prisoner at the end of the sentence with no supervision.

d. **Personal values of board members**: Parole decisions are also influenced by the personal values and philosophies of individual board members. Such factors as attendance at chapel or Sunday school, personal habits such as teeth brushing, and hairstyle may therefore affect an inmate's chances for release on parole.

e. **Economic factors**: A parole board may feel constrained to release prisoners on parole for budgetary or other economic reasons. In this regard, the "body crunch" resulting from excessively large inmate populations in most prisons has created pressure to reduce crowded conditions; and the granting of additional (or earlier) paroles has been seized on as one means of alleviating the problem.

f. **Political considerations**: Finally, it is an unfortunate fact of life that parole decisions with respect to certain prisoners may be made on the basis of political considerations. A well-known inmate, or one who has powerful friends, may have an advantage in obtaining parole; and, conversely, a victim with powerful friends can do much to block a parole.

2. **Information Base for Parole Decision Making**: Whatever the particular criteria applied by a parole board in selecting inmates for release, a full range of information is required for effective decision making.

a. **Pre-parole progress report**: In most cases, the staff of the prison or correctional institution prepares a progress report on inmates for submission to the parole board. This report typically includes a summary of the inmate's offense and basic problems, the institutional programs in which he or she has participated, a suggested plan for parole (including information about employment and residence), and a staff recommendation for or against parole. The information in the pre-parole report should be accurate and complete. This is frequently not the case, however, for the following reasons:

(1) **Staff shortages**: In many institutions, a shortage of institutional staff—including the professionals who compile most of the available information on inmates—limits the access of parole boards to needed information.

(2) **Excessive caseloads**: Similarly, excessive caseloads often cause caseworkers to prepare reports based on a short interview with the prisoner and meager institutional records. This often results in highly stereotyped reports that fail to deal with the unique aspects of each case.

(3) **Lack of diagnostic reports**: Psychiatric reports and other information on the treatment of inmates may not be available, leaving the parole board with a data base limited to the inmate's criminal and prison conduct records.

(4) **Inadequate information from judicial process**: Since they are intended for a different purpose, official statements by judges or prosecutors at the time of trial often have little value in parole decision making.

(5) **Biased information from institutional records**: Finally, even where substantial information is compiled in the pre-parole report, it frequently reflects the judgments of institutional personnel whose main concern is the inmate's ability to adjust to prison life (and who may be less interested in how the inmate will adjust to the community outside the prison).

b. **Data base recommended by Model Penal Code**: The Model Penal Code suggests that parole boards evaluate each inmate on the basis of the following comprehensive information:

(1) **Report of institutional staff**: The file on each inmate should contain a report by the institutional staff, detailing the inmate's personality, social history, and adjustment to authority. The report should also include any comments that the institutional staff may wish to make concerning the advisability of releasing the inmate on parole.

(2) **Past criminal record**: An inmate's file should contain all official reports of his or her prior criminal record, plus reports of any previous probation or parole experience.

(3) **Pre-sentence investigation**: The parole board should have access to the pre-sentence investigation report of the sentencing court.

(4) **Recommendations of sentencing court**: Likewise, any recommendations made by the judge or prosecutor at the time of sentencing should be available to the board.

(5) **Medical reports**: Complete reports of any physical or psychiatric examinations of the prisoner should be included in his or her file for review by the paroling authority.

(6) **Parole plan**: A detailed parole plan, including information on future employment and living arrangements, should be developed for every inmate being considered for parole.

(7) **Other relevant information**: Finally, any other information relevant to parole may be included in the prisoner's file, to be drawn on by the board as needed. This might include material submitted by the inmate, his or her attorney, the victim, or other persons interested in the matter.[9]

c. **Parole prediction tables**: As developed for parole decision making, prediction tables involve statistics on the behavior of various types of offenders after release from incarceration.[10]

(1) **Data base for prediction tables:** The data used to compile prediction tables come from several sources, including pre-sentence investigations, classification summaries, and supervision reports. A table is only as sound as the information in its data base, so staff competence is essential to the proper development and use of such material.

(2) **Advantages of prediction tables:** Prediction tables help to make more concrete the factors relevant to parole decision making and act as a valuable check on "gut-feeling" or intuitive hunches by board members. Such hunches are necessarily subjective and vary from case to case, creating inconsistencies and leading to criticism of the parole process.

Some critics see a danger in relying exclusively on tables arrived at by statistical methods, citing the axiom that "a machine that can predict without touching can err without guilt." However, even these critics agree that prediction tables can be helpful in screening out cases that are obviously inappropriate for parole, thereby freeing the board from what would otherwise be a great deal of unnecessary review and permitting it to concentrate on a careful examination of the remaining cases.

3. **Decision Guidelines of United States Parole Board:** The United States Board of Parole has devised a procedure intended both to structure the federal parole process and to make paroling policy explicit. The technique involves the development of decision guidelines through identifying selection factors and assigning a weight to each such factor. Since the guidelines clearly articulate the criteria being used in the decision-making process, they provide the inmate, the sentencing judge, and the general public with a better understanding of that process.[11]

4. **Decision Guidelines in State Procedures:** The advantages of explicit guidelines in the decision-making process are also being recognized by state parole authorities. Louisiana, Minnesota, Missouri, New Jersey, North Carolina, Virginia, and Washington are among the jurisdictions that have developed formalized guidelines or are in the process of doing so; and there is considerable interest in other states as well.

F. REVIEW OF PAROLE DECISIONS

1. **Underlying Theories of Parole Board Discretion:** The discretion given to parole boards in granting, denying, or revoking parole stems from an assumption that the board is the entity best equipped to make these decisions affecting individual inmates and society at large. As a matter of statutory authority, such discretion tends to be grounded in one of three legal theories of parole—the grace theory, the contract theory, or the custody theory.[12]

   a. **"Grace" theory:** The grace theory views parole as a gift from the executive branch of government—that is, a conditional privilege which may be taken away if the parole board believes it should be revoked. Under the grace theory, such executive discretion is not subject to judicial review.

   b. **"Contract" theory:** The contract theory visualizes parole as an agreement between the state and the inmate. Failure to abide by the terms of the agreement is thus a proper ground for rescinding parole.

c. **"Custody" theory**: Under this theory, the parolee is viewed as being in legal custody—that is, an inmate serving part of his or her sentence outside the prison. Accordingly, the rights of a parolee are limited owing to his or her continuing status as a prisoner.

2. **Judicial Review of Parole Decisions**: The parole board is an administrative body within the executive branch; and judicial review of parole decisions therefore differs from review of decisions made by a lower court.

   a. **No automatic right to review**: As a general rule, the courts do not interfere with the exercise of board discretion in parole release decisions. The right to be considered for parole and the timing of the parole hearing usually are held to be matters for the paroling authority (subject to any applicable statutory requirements).

      Example: In *Greenholtz* v. *Inmates of Nebraska Penal & Correctional Complex*, the U.S. Supreme Court held that there is no constitutional or inherent right to be released before the expiration of a valid sentence.[13] This decision was in accord with a number of lower federal court opinions refusing to interfere in the parole decision-making process on the grounds that parole is not a right but a matter of grace.[14]

   b. **Review for abuse of discretion**: However, parole decisions are subject to judicial review for abuse of discretion by the paroling authority. Such review is important, because it upholds the integrity of the decision-making process and serves as a deterrent to abuse. In particular, the courts have been asked to uphold the due-process rights of inmates in parole proceedings.

      (1) **Basic standard for review**: The scope of judicial review for discretionary actions like parole decisions involves determining whether the agency acted within the scope of its authority; whether its action was "arbitrary, capricious, an abuse of discretion, or otherwise not in accordance with law"; and whether the agency followed the necessary procedural requirements. However, the U.S. Supreme Court has held that this standard is a narrow one, and that the court is *not* empowered to substitute its judgment for that of the agency.[15]

      (2) **Record for review**: Obviously, effective judicial review depends on an adequate record of the parole hearing; and thorough records help to ensure unbiased decisions by the board. As of 1976, some twenty-one jurisdictions required written, verbatim records of parole release hearings.[16]

         A related requirement for effective review is an explanation by the paroling authority of the reasons for denial of parole. As of 1976, thirty-four states and the federal parole system required that both a written and an oral explanation of the reasons for denial be given to the inmate in question. Twelve other states require only a written explanation, and two require only an oral statement from the board. In three states, the paroling authority need give no explanation (written or oral) for denying release on parole.[17]

   c. **Representation by counsel at parole hearing**: It has been argued that inmates are entitled to an attorney at parole hearings, on the theory that counsel can help to gather and verify information on the prospective parolee and thus assist the board (and the inmate) in arriving at informed decisions. Twenty-one states permit the inmate to have an attorney present at the hearing; and of these, six also provide for appointment of counsel in certain situations.[18]

(1) **No right to counsel**: Aside from these statutory provisions, however, there appears to be no due-process right to counsel at parole release hearings. The courts have found that such hearings are not adversary proceedings, and hence that counsel need not be appointed or even allowed to attend.[19]

(2) **Compare—parole revocation hearings**: Note that a parolee *may* have a constitutional right to an attorney (including appointed counsel, for indigents) in parole revocation, as opposed to parole release, hearings. This subject is discussed in Chapter VI.

3. **Administrative Appeal of Parole Decisions**: Administrative appeal involves an internal review of parole release decisions by the paroling authority itself. In its *Report on Corrections*, the National Advisory Commission on Criminal Justice Standards and Goals has stressed the need for internal appeal procedures as an alternative to judicial review and as a means of strengthening the image of fairness and propriety in the decision-making process. Among other things, this system can help to relieve crowded court calendars by reducing the number of cases in which judicial review of parole decisions is sought.[20]

a. **Structure proposed by National Advisory Commission**: The National Advisory Commission has suggested standards for a parole structure that would enhance the initial decision-making process as well as provide for administrative appeal. The proposed structure would allow parole board members to devote most of their attention to policy development and appeals, leaving most case-by-case decision making to hearing examiners. Such examiners in turn would be delegated the power to grant, deny, or revoke parole subject to the rules and policies of the board.

(1) **Duties of parole board**: Under the proposed plan, the parole board would be directly responsible for developing and articulating policy, for acting on appeals of hearing examiner decisions, and for issuing and signing warrants to arrest and hold alleged parole violators.

(2) **Duties of hearing examiners**: Hearing examiners in the NAC plan would hear parole release and revocation cases and make initial decisions according to the specific policies and criteria of the parole board. The report of the hearing examiner, containing a transcript of the hearing and the evidence considered, would constitute the exclusive record of the hearing; and the examiner's decision would be final unless appealed by the correctional authority or the offender within five days.

(3) **Scope of review on appeal**: In the event of an appeal, the parole board would review the case on the basis of whether there was substantial evidence in the report to support the examiner's finding and whether the finding was correct as a matter of law.

(4) **Sensitivity to needs of correctional institutions**: In carrying out their respective functions, both parole board members and hearing examiners should have a close understanding of correctional institutions, the nature of their programs, and the activities of offenders.

(5) **"Combined" functions for smaller jurisdictions**: While the parole authority in large states would presumably have a staff of full-time hearing examiners appointed under civil service regulations, the NAC recognizes that parole boards in smaller states may have to assume responsibility for all the duties just discussed. Even so, the board should establish clearly defined and distinct procedures for policy development, hearings, and appeals.[21]

b. **Implementation of NAC proposal**

(1) **Pilot project**: In 1972, the United States Board of Parole began a pilot project in five federal institutions in the northeastern United States, using the National Advisory Commission standards as a model. Innovative features of the project included the use of two-member panels of hearing examiners, the structuring of discretion through the use of explicit decision-making guidelines, preparation of written reasons for parole denial, provision for limited representation by counsel at release hearings, and a two-step administrative appeal process. Under the latter process, an inmate could delay thirty days in appealing an adverse decision if significant information in existence at the time of the hearing was not considered, or if the reasons given for denial of parole did not adequately support the decision made.[22]

(2) **Full-scale plan**: On the basis of experience with the pilot project, the U.S. Board of Parole established a plan for full-scale reorganization of the federal parole process along similar lines. The plan was approved by the United States Attorney General in August 1973; and in January 1974, Congress passed a supplemental appropriation bill to provide necessary funding.[23]

c. **Present scope of administrative appeal**: As of 1976, twenty-three states plus the United States Parole Commission offered inmates an opportunity to appeal the decision in parole release hearings.[24]

4. **Overview of Parole Hearing Process**: Table 5.2 indicates the relevant characteristics of the parole hearing process in the federal system, the fifty states, and the District of Columbia.

Table 5.2

Characteristics of Parole Release Hearings, by Jurisdiction, 1976

Jurisdiction	Attorney Permitted	Attorney Appointed	Witnesses Permitted	When Informed of the Decision	Oral Explanation of Decision	Written Explanation of Decision	Verbatim Record	Appeal Permitted
Alabama	No	X	No	Immediately and in prison	Yes	Yes	No	Yes
Alaska	Yes	Yes	No[a]	Immediately after hearing by institutional staff	Yes	Yes	No	Yes
Arizona	Yes	No	Yes	In writing, within 5 days	No	Yes	No	No
Arkansas	Yes	X	Yes	In writing, within 48 hours	Yes	Yes	No	No
California Adult	No	X	No	Immediately and in person	Yes	Yes[b]	No	Yes
Colorado	No	X	No	In writing, as soon as the full board considers the case	No	No[c]	Yes	No
Connecticut	No	X	No	Immediately and in person	Yes[b]	Yes[b]	Yes	No
Delaware	No	X	No	In writing, at the end of the hearing day	No	Yes	No	No
District of Columbia	No	X	No	In writing within 7 days	Yes	Yes	Yes	Yes
Florida	No	X	No	Immediately and in person	Yes	Yes	Yes	No
Georgia	X	X	X	X	Yes	Yes[b]	X	Yes
Hawaii	Yes	Yes	Yes	Within 30 days	Yes	Yes	Yes	Yes
Idaho	Yes	No	Yes	Immediately and in person	Yes	No	Yes	No
Illinois	Yes	No	Yes	In writing, following the hearing	No	Yes	Yes	Yes
Indiana	No	X	No	Immediately and in person	Yes	Yes	No	No
Iowa	No	X	No	Immediately and in person	Yes[d]	Yes	No	Yes
Kansas	Yes	No	Yes[e]	In writing within a few days	No	Yes	No	Yes
Kentucky	Yes	Yes	No[f]	In writing, same day	No	Yes	No	No
Louisiana	Yes	No	Yes	Immediately and in person	Yes	Yes	No	Yes
Maine	No	X	Yes	Immediately and in person	Yes	Yes	No	Yes
Maryland	No	X	No	Immediately and in person	Yes	Yes	Yes	Yes
Massachusetts	No	X	No	Immediately and in person	Yes	Yes[b]	No	Yes
Michigan	No	X	No	Immediately and in person	Yes	Yes	No	No
Minnesota	No	X	No	Immediately and in person	Yes	Yes	No	No
Mississippi	No	X	Yes	By mail, after the hearing	No	Yes	Yes	No
Missouri	No	X	No	By mail, within 4 days	Yes	Yes	Yes	Yes
Montana	No	X	No	In writing, immediately after hearing	No	Yes	No	Yes
Nebraska	Yes	No	Yes	Immediately and in person	Yes	Yes	Yes	No
Nevada	No	X	No	Same day, institutional counselor	Yes	No	No	No
New Hampshire	Yes	No	Yes	Immediately and in person	Yes	Yes	Yes	Yes
New Jersey	Yes	No	No	In writing, within 3 to 4 weeks	Yes	Yes	No	Yes
New Mexico	No	X	No	Immediately and in person	Yes	Yes	No	Yes
New York	No	X	No	In writing, within 24 hours	No	Yes	Yes	Yes
North Carolina	Yes	No	Yes	Within 1 to 3 weeks	No	Yes	No	No
North Dakota	Yes	No	Yes	Same day, by board members	Yes	Yes	Yes	No
Ohio	No	X	No	End of hearing, by board members	Yes	Yes	No	Yes
Oklahoma	Yes	No	Yes	Immediately after hearing, institutional counselor	No	No	No	No
Oregon	No	X	No	Immediately and in person	Yes	Yes	Yes	No
Pennsylvania	No	X	No	Same day, board members	Yes	Yes	No	No
Rhode Island	Yes	Yes	No	Same day, classification officer	Yes	Yes	No	No
South Carolina	Yes	No	Yes	By mail, after the hearing	No	Yes	Yes	No
South Dakota	Yes	No	Yes	In writing, after the hearing	No	No	No	No
Tennessee	Yes	No	Yes	Immediately and in person	Yes	Yes	No	Yes
Texas	X	X	X	X	Yes	Yes	X	No
Utah	No	X	Yes	Immediately and in person	Yes	Yes	Yes	No
Vermont	Yes	Yes	Yes	Immediately and in person	Yes	Yes	Yes	Yes
Virginia	No	X	No	In writing, after the hearing	No	Yes	No	Yes
Washington	No	X	No	Immediately and in person	Yes	Yes	No	No
West Virginia	No	X	No	Immediately and in person	Yes	Yes	Yes	No
Wisconsin	No	X	No	Immediately and in person	Yes	Yes	Yes	No
Wyoming	Yes	Yes	Yes	In writing, after the hearing	No	Yes	Yes	No
U.S. Parole Commission	No	X	No	Tentative—immediately and in person; final—within 21 days	Yes	Yes	Yes	Yes

[a]Generally not without the advance permission of the board.
[b]Denial only.
[c]Denials are accompanied by a memo to staff; staff may then suggest to the inmate the reasons for the decision.
[d]If parole is granted.
[e]With advance permission from the Authority.
[f]Unusual, but sometimes permitted, with the permission of the board.

Source: Vincent O'Leary and Kathleen J. Hanrahan, *Parole Systems in the United States: A Detailed Description of Their Structure and Procedures*, 3rd ed. (Hackensack, N.J.: National Council on Crime and Delinquency, 1977), pp. 42–47, Summary Tables 5 and 6.

NOTES

[1] National Advisory Commission on Criminal Justice Standards and Goals, *Corrections* (Washington, D.C.: U.S. Government Printing Office, 1973), p. 389.

[2] *Ibid.*, pp. 392-93.

[3] *Ibid.*, pp. 197-209.

[4] *Ibid.*, p. 400.

[5] Vincent O'Leary and Kathleen J. Hanrahan, *Parole Systems in the United States: A Detailed Description of Their Structure and Procedures*, 3rd ed. (Hackensack, N.J.: National Council on Crime and Delinquency, 1977), pp. 42-47.

[6] Robert O. Dawson, *Sentencing: The Decision as to Type, Length, and Conditions of Sentence* (Boston: Little, Brown, 1969).

[7] George G. Killinger, Hazel B. Kerper, and Paul F. Cromwell, Jr., *Probation and Parole in the Criminal Justice System* (St. Paul, Minn.: West Publishing Co., 1976), pp. 250-51.

[8] National Advisory Commission on Criminal Justice Standards and Goals, pp. 393-95.

[9] American Law Institute, *Model Penal Code*, Section 305.10, pp. 292-93, Philadelphia, 1961.

[10] Daniel Glaser, *The Effectiveness of a Prison and Parole System* (Indianapolis, Ind.: Bobbs-Merrill, 1969), p. 207.

[11] Section 2.20 Paroling Policy Guidelines, *Federal Register*, 41: 173, Friday, Sept. 3, 1976.

[12] Michael Gottesman and Lewis J. Hecker, "Parole: A Critique of Its Legal Foundations," in Robert M. Carter and Leslie T. Wilkins, eds., *Probation and Parole: Selected Readings* (New York: Wiley, 1970).

[13] *Greenholtz* v. *Inmates of Nebraska Penal & Correctional Complex*, 442 U.S.1 (1979).

[14] See *Tarlton* v. *Clark*, 441 F. 2d 384 (5th Cir. 1971); *United States* v. *Frederick*, 405 F. 2d 129 (3rd Cir. 1968); *Brest* v. *Ciconce*, 371 F. 2d 981 (8th Cir. 1967); *Walker* v. *Taylor*, 338 F. 2d 945 (10th Cir. 1964).

[15] *Citizens to Preserve Overton Park* v. *Volpe*, 401 U.S. 402 (1971).

[16] O'Leary and Hanrahan, pp. 42-47.

[17] *Ibid.*

[18] *Ibid.*

[19] See, for example, *Menechino* v. *Oswald*, 430 F. 2d 403 (2d Cir. 1970).

[20] National Advisory Commission on Criminal Justice Standards and Goals, pp. 397-98.

[21] *Ibid.*, p. 417.

[22] Hoffman, Peter B. and De Gostin, Lucille K., "Parole Decision-Making: Structuring Discretion," *Federal Probation*, 38: 4 (December 1974), 7-15.

[23] *Federal Register*, Part II, 38: 184 (September 24, 1973), and *Federal Register*, Part III, 38: 222 (November 19, 1973).

[24] O'Leary and Hanrahan, pp. 42-47.

VI. THE SUPERVISION PROCESS IN PROBATION AND PAROLE

A. PURPOSE AND NATURE OF SUPERVISION

Supervision is the heart of probation and parole work, since it is the process through which the two major goals of probation and parole—protection of society and successful reintegration of offenders—are achieved. For the most part, probation and parole supervision are similar; but there are some differences reflecting the divergent needs and experiences of probationers and parolees.

1. **Functional Areas of Supervision:** In meeting its twofold purpose of serving society and the offender, the supervision process involves three distinct but interrelated sets of functions: investigation, treatment, and surveillance.

   a. **Investigation:** The investigative phase of probation and parole supervision requires gathering information about the offender and his or her life situation. Such information aids in the decision-making process and helps to plan an effective rehabilitation program for the offender.

   b. **Treatment:** In probation and parole work, the word "treatment" is used in a broad sense to refer to all policies and actions designed to restore the offender to a productive, meaningful, and law-abiding role in society. Casework, individual and group counseling, therapy programs, and effective mobilization of community resources are included in this facet of supervision.

   c. **Surveillance:** The supervision process involves an important surveillance function. Such surveillance encompasses all policies and actions aimed at securing the offender's compliance with the law and with the conditions of his or her release, and is designed to protect the public by ensuring proper behavior on the part of probationers and parolees.

2. **Similarities in Probation and Parole Supervision:** In many respects, the supervision process is the same in probation and parole programs. In both, supervision has the objective of restoring offenders to meaningful lives while protecting society, and seeks to attain that objective through similar means. Treatment techniques common to both include casework, individual and group counseling, therapeutic programs, and community service brokerage; and the surveillance function of both programs is designed to enforce conditions of release and help offenders meet those conditions. As a result, probation and parole supervision in the federal system and in a number of state systems is handled by a single agency.

3. **Differences in Supervising Probationers and Parolees:** Although the processes involved in probation and parole supervision are similar, the differences between probationers and parolees still require somewhat different emphases in the two programs. The most significant differences (noted in Chapter I) relate to prior criminal records, adjustment problems, and societal reactions.

   a. **Prior criminal records:** Parolees often have extensive criminal records and have been incarcerated in prison prior to their release (thus increasing the chance of a "criminal" identification). Probationers, in contrast, are less likely to have prior records or to have committed serious crimes; and the supervisory process for these offenders may therefore stress treatment more than surveillance.

b. **Adjustment needs**: Given their incarceration experience and estrangement from family and friends, parolees often have difficulty adjusting to the outside world and thus require careful supervision and counseling. Conversely, probationers usually have not suffered these dislocations (or at least not to the same degree); and their adjustment to the community tends to be considerably easier.

c. **Societal reaction**: Finally, parolees are frequently labeled "ex-cons," thereby incurring public distrust and a much more difficult readjustment to society. This situation requires greater attention from the supervising authority than does that of probationers, who typically have not served time and are regarded as less serious offenders by the very fact that they "got probation."

B. PRE-RELEASE CASEWORK

1. **Parole Investigations**: When a prison inmate is eligible for parole, the parole officer often has the responsibility of investigating the feasibility of release for that inmate. The officer's report is then reviewed by the parole board in determining whether or not to grant parole. A pre-release investigation typically consists of the following tasks:

   a. **Review of case history**: The investigating officer first checks the inmate's case history to make sure that the facts concerning the case are accurate and up-to-date.

   b. **Review of institutional record**: A check of the prisoner's institutional record is next made in order to determine how well he or she has adjusted to life in a correctional institution.

   c. **Consultation with judicial and law-enforcement officers**: The parole officer may also wish to notify or check with the judge who tried the inmate, the district attorney who prosecuted the case, and the sheriff of the jurisdiction in which the inmate wishes to be paroled. The opinions of these individuals on the desirability of parole are important; and it may be advisable to have the parolee released elsewhere (or in some cases not released at all) if strong objections are voiced.

   d. **Investigation of proposed residence**: The parole officer likewise investigates the inmate's proposed place of residence to make certain that it is suitable for a parolee. The investigation will include an examination of the inmate's family and domestic life for any conditions that might aid or discourage a successful parole. If the inmate has no family, or if a return to his or her family is considered not to be desirable, an alternative such as placement in a halfway house will be arranged.

   e. **Investigation of proposed employment**: Finally, it is the responsibility of the parole officer to verify the employment plan to ensure that the inmate will have suitable work should he or she be paroled.

2. **Probation Plan**: The probation officer plays a critical role in the granting of probation, since he or she compiles the social history report (for juveniles) or pre-sentence investigation report (for adults) to aid the court in making appropriate dispositions. (The characteristics

of pre-probation investigations were discussed in Chapter III, and should be reviewed at this point.)

C. MANAGEMENT OF PROBATION AND PAROLE SUPERVISION

1. **Need for Immediate Contact with Offender:** The supervising authority must establish contact with the probationer or parolee as soon as possible after the offender is released. Indeed, this contact and communication should be made prior to release whenever possible.

   a. **Purpose of early contact:** More often than not, a newly released offender understands little of the process under which release occurs. The probation or parole officer should take the opportunity to explain the concept and answer any questions the offender may have. The officer should also establish a relationship as the offender's supervisor and discuss the nature, goals, and requirements of release with the offender at the earliest possible time. Among other things, the officer must explain the conditions of release (discussed later in this chapter) and the consequences of violating such conditions. This involves more than just reading the terms of release: The officer must make sure that the offender understands the conditions and fully agrees to observe them.

   b. **Consequences of delay in establishing contact:** Any delay between the time an offender is released on probation or parole and the first contact with the supervising officer undermines the goals of the release. The anxiety and uncertainty that an offender typically feels prior to receiving probation or parole may be replaced by a feeling that he or she is "free" and need no longer be concerned about his or her behavior. Thus, it is important that the supervising officer impress upon the newly released probationer or parolee *at the outset* that the release is subject to the conditions imposed with it.

2. **Planning the Supervision Program:** An individual supervision program for the released offender should be worked out at the first meeting between the offender and the officer. Problems should be assessed at that time and plans developed to maximize the chances of a successful reintegration. Family, school, or career goals of the offender are an especially important part of developing a reintegration program.

   a. **Participation of offender in planning program:** It is important that the probationer or parolee have a voice in the development of his or her supervision program. This will help the offender to understand fully the rationale behind any plan for his or her behavior, and to realize that the responsibility for making major life decisions cannot be shifted entirely to someone else. The supervising officer and the offender should explore the latter's individual needs, and the officer should encourage the client to think carefully about his or her future.

   b. **Probation plan based on personality studies:** One useful approach in designing effective supervision plans is to study the personality characteristics of particular offender groups, since an understanding of the personality constructs from which certain behavior flows makes it possible to tailor programs to the unique strengths and weaknesses of the released offender. A study by James Moore and Robert Shearer,[1] discussed previously in Chapter III, suggests that the design of probation (and possibly parole) programs be based on an appraisal of three personality characteristics: manipulative behavior, self-control, and anxiety. The behavior manifested in these three areas can significantly affect the probation process; and taking them into account may therefore enhance the effectiveness of probation. As a result of their study, Moore and Shearer recommend the following two-stage probation plan:

(1) **Stage one**: The initial program for a probated felon would involve a highly structured written contract in which behavioral objectives, expectations, and consequences are clearly articulated and a timetable for assessing progress is set forth. The probation officer would assume control over all decision making in this first stage, making sure to assert his or her power in an evenhanded, consistent manner. At the same time, every effort would be made to establish unambiguous lines of communication between the offender and the supervising officer.

(2) **Stage two**: The initial probation phase would evolve into a second stage conditioned by the probationer's behavior. Here, "mutual agreement" programming—in which the probationer assumes a role in decision making and takes responsibility for the consequences of these decisions—might be employed; and short, intermediate, and long-term goals with clear, written reward schedules could be established. Supervision could then be decreased as the probationer assumed an increasing role in his or her reintegration program.

3. **Conditions of Release**: A fundamental part of the supervisory process in probation and parole are the requirements imposed by the sentencing court or paroling authority to control the offender's conduct after release.

   a. **Purpose of conditions**: Conditions of release are primarily important for the surveillance function of supervision. In this respect, they serve as guidelines for both the released offender and the supervising officer.

   (1) **Guidelines for offender**: For the offender, release on probation or parole is a testing period during which he or she must demonstrate the capacity to readjust to the community as a law-abiding citizen. The conditions attached to release aid the parolee or probationer in developing behavior consistent with reintegration.

   (2) **Guidelines for officers**: At the same time, the established conditions aid the probation or parole officer in that they prescribe the minimum standard of conduct that he or she is expected to enforce.

   b. **Criteria for effective release conditions**: In order for conditions of release to serve as effective guidelines, they must meet certain criteria:

   (1) **Requirements should be realistic**: The conditions imposed by the court or paroling authority should be realistic and enforceable. Such requirements lose their meaning if they are not reasonable, practical, and within the purview of the law.

   (2) **Requirements should be "individualized"**: Conditions of probation or parole should be tailored as closely as possible to the needs of the offender in question, with the recognition that offenders encompass a broad spectrum with widely divergent needs, abilities, and life situations.

   (3) **Requirements must be properly administered**: If the conditions attached to release on

probation or parole are to serve as guidelines for acceptable behavior, they must be administered by the supervising agency in a fair and sensible manner. The aim should be to help the offender develop a normal lifestyle, rather than to enforce restrictions as a type of further punishment.

c. **Typical conditions of release:** Requirements governing release are basically the same for probation and parole, and have changed very little over the years. A typical set of conditions would require the released offender to do the following:

(1) Obtain permission to:

    (a) change job or residence,

    (b) leave the jurisdiction,

    (c) marry,

    (d) assume any substantial indebtedness,

    (e) buy or operate an automobile, or

    (f) buy or possess firearms.

(2) Maintain steady employment.

(3) Support dependents, if any.

(4) Report earnings and debts accurately.

(5) Avoid the excessive use of intoxicants.

(6) Avoid disreputable places and associates.

(7) Keep reasonable hours (or a specified curfew).

(8) Submit written reports.

(9) Comply with all instructions of the supervising officer.

d. **Current trends in release requirements:** In recent years, there has been a move toward reducing the number of conditions imposed on probationers and parolees and making the conditions that are imposed more relevant to the individual offender. This trend can be largely attributed to court decisions striking down conditions on the ground that they were impossible, unreasonable, unfair, or all three.

(1) **Examples of conditions held to be improper:** The following examples indicate the types of release conditions being scrutinized by the courts:

    (a) A juvenile court order requiring attendance at church and Sunday school has been held unconstitutional under the First Amendment, since "no civil authority has the right to require anyone to accept or reject any religious belief or to contribute any support thereto."[2]

(b) A requirement that a defendant donate blood to the Red Cross has been declared illegal.[3]

(c) Similarly, banishment as a condition of probation has been held void and unenforceable.[4]

(d) As a general matter, courts tolerate the imposition of more stringent conditions on parolees than probationers, since a parolee is "constructively a prisoner of the state" (that is, still in constructive custody while released on parole).[5]

(2) **Release requirements in state of Washington:** Perhaps the greatest changes in imposition of release requirements have occurred in the state of Washington.

(a) **Standard conditions:** The standard conditions of parole imposed on Washington inmates have been reduced to four requirements:

1) Obey all laws.

2) Secure permission from a parole officer before leaving the state.

3) Report to the assigned parole officer.

4) Obey any written instructions issued by the parole officer.

(b) **Additional conditions optional:** The State Board of Parole may impose additional conditions in specific cases as it deems appropriate; conditions also may be added from time to time on the request of the parole officer.

(c) **Advantages of Washington system:** The Washington system is advantageous to the parolee and to the supervising officer. Both parties know which conditions must be enforced (as opposed to the typical situation, in which numerous "standard" conditions are purportedly applied to every released offender); and the parolee avoids the unnecessary anxiety of attempting to comply with vague or ambiguous rules.

4. **Appropriate Amount of Supervision**

a. **Basic levels or degrees of supervision:** Many departments provide more than one level or degree of supervision for released offenders. The typical system involves three basic levels: maximum, medium, and minimum.

(1) **Maximum supervision:** Maximum or special supervision is appropriate for all newly released offenders and in cases where there is deemed to be a substantial risk of further criminal activity. This level of supervision necessitates weekly personal contacts between the offender and the supervisor; in some instances, more frequent contacts are required. At least some of these contacts occur at the offender's residence so that the supervising officer may observe the circumstances in which the client is functioning.

A client with serious employment difficulties will frequently be placed in the maximum-supervision category so that close attention to his or her work experience can be maintained. In these situations, the supervising officer must make clear to the client exactly what is expected.

(2) **Medium supervision:** A majority of clients require regular contact with their supervising officers no more than once or twice a month (although extra supervision may be needed at times). At this level, reporting is scheduled so that the offender can meet responsibilities at work or school.

(3) **Minimum supervision:** When an offender has demonstrated a readjustment to community life through his or her ability to keep a job, maintain a satisfactory personal life, and fulfill the obligation to report to the supervising agency, he or she may be placed on "minimum supervision" status. This may allow the client to report even less frequently (and perhaps by mail), since it is assumed that the offender has substantially fulfilled the objectives of the initial supervision program.

Increasing use of minimum supervision: There is a pronounced tendency toward minimum supervision in many departments today. The trend is especially noticeable in rural areas, where as much as one-third of the total caseload may be handled in this manner. Experience has shown that relatively few problems or failures are encountered with this level of supervision (when applied judiciously); and it permits the supervisory staff to devote more time to offenders more in need of their attention.

(4) **Shifts in levels of supervision:** As the preceding discussion indicates, the level of supervision for a particular offender can be increased or decreased as the situation warrants. In such cases, the supervising officer will need to revise the offender's program plan as needed.

(a) **Case "promotion":** Department administrators should encourage their staffs to move cases from more intense levels of supervision to less intense levels whenever appropriate, since this allows supervising officers to spend more time with cases needing more attention.

(b) **Case "demotion":** At the same time, of course, a released offender who fails to meet the requirements of the assigned level of supervision generally should be placed in a program calling for more intensive supervision.

b. **Early discharge:** Another procedure especially applicable to probation is early discharge. Indeed, reliance on this procedure may be expected to increase as more and more offenders are processed through the criminal justice system.

(1) **Advantages:** Early discharge makes it possible to accommodate "intensive care" cases more easily. In addition, the possibility of discharge may help to motivate offenders in readjusting properly to society.

(2) **Timing of discharge:** A released offender may properly be considered for early discharge when he or she performs well under minimum supervision and meets the applicable statutory requirements for such discharge.

5. **Proper Caseload Allocation:** An important issue confronting probation and parole administrators is caseload size: that is, what is the maximum number of released offenders that can be supervised properly by one officer?

a. **Traditional caseload standard:** Historically, a caseload of fifty offenders for each supervising officer was assumed to be the optimum and was rarely questioned.[6] In recent years, however, this "caseload" standard has been more carefully scrutinized, particularly with respect to the relationship between caseload size and recidivism (tendency to commit new offenses and infractions of the conditions of release).

(1) **Results of San Francisco Project:** In 1964, the United States Probation Office for the Northern District of California began a study on caseload size, examining the results of four levels of caseload supervision.[7]

(a) **Caseloads studied:** The levels of supervision examined in the San Francisco Project ranged from "intensive" to "minimum." An "intensive" caseload was one in which the officer was assigned one pre-sentence investigation and twenty cases for supervision per month; the "ideal" caseload was composed of two PSI's and forty cases for supervision per month; a "regular" caseload comprised eight PSI's and eighty to one hundred supervision cases per month; and a "minimum" caseload consisted of up to 350 cases each month but involved no PSI's and only written contact with offenders.

(b) **Results:** The only important difference among these four levels of supervision noted by the San Francisco study was that "intensive" caseloads produced far more technical violations by offenders than did the other caseload levels. Presumably, this resulted from the increased surveillance possible in smaller intensive caseloads.

(2) **Findings in other studies:** Additional studies such as the Saginaw Project[8] suggest that mere caseload size is not an important factor in assessing the likelihood of recidivism among released offenders. Revocation policies, behavior of probation or parole officers, and the type of supervision services provided all appear to be more significant than caseload size in this respect.

(3) **Position of National Advisory Commission:** In its 1973 study on corrections, the National Advisory Commission on Criminal Justice Standards and Goals emphasized two points in discussing the traditional caseload standard:[9]

(a) **Caseload standard as "handy excuse":** First, the NAC noted that the caseload standard frequently became an excuse used by officers with large caseloads to explain problems in supervising released offenders effectively. Likewise, the standard was frequently advanced as a bargaining point in seeking larger supervisory staffs and an increased budget for probation or parole departments.

(b) **Reduced caseload size should not be an end in itself:** Secondly, the NAC observed that where reducing caseload size had become an end in itself (as was frequently the case), the results were disappointing. As noted above, the increased surveillance possible with small caseloads might actually increase violation rates without measurable improvement in the adjustment process for offenders.

(4) **Consensus of studies**: The caseload standard of fifty cases per officer was an attempt to provide sufficient time for a traditional casework approach to each offender's needs, a small caseload ostensibly having a direct relationship to effective supervision. However, the foregoing studies have demonstrated that assignments for supervisory officers should be based on more than mere numbers of cases. Among other factors, the offender, the officer, and the type of treatment being proposed should be considered.

b. **Current trend to "workload" standard**: The caseload standard of fifty was first suggested in 1917.[10] Fifty years later, in 1967, the President's Commission on Law Enforcement and Administration of Justice recommended that supervisory assignments be based on a workload, rather than caseload, standard.[11] Rather than merely relying on a case count, the workload concept—based on procedures of differential association such as case classification, matching of offenders with type of service to be offered, and the like—emphasizes cases that most need supervision.

(1) **Flexibility of workload standard**: The workload concept is flexible enough to assess and control case assignments for several different types of situations, depending on levels of supervision, types of supervision, and defined supervisory tasks.

(a) **Levels of supervision**: In some departments, officers are assigned cases on only one supervision level. Minimum-supervision caseloads in such departments are large, while medium- and maximum-supervision loads are progressively smaller in size. Other departments, however, may assign caseloads on more than one supervision level, permitting continuous supervision by one officer as the offender is promoted (or demoted) from one level to another. Since it is not based on a fixed number of case assignments, the workload standard permits different levels of supervision to be considered in establishing assignments.

(b) **Types of supervision**: The type of supervision used by probation or parole authorities likewise may vary from the traditional one-to-one casework approach to the resource-broker or department-team approach. Whatever the focus, the workload concept makes it possible to establish flexible criteria in developing staff assignments.

(c) **Functional duties**: Some members of the probation or parole staff may concentrate solely on investigative work (such as social histories, pre-sentence investigations, or pre-parole examinations), while others may only supervise released offenders. Here again, the workload concept makes it possible to apportion functional tasks in a fair and appropriate manner.

(2) **Assessing department workloads—the Texas Master Plan Survey**: In 1976, the administrators of probation programs in the state of Texas were asked to estimate the amounts of time spent by their respective staffs in the several areas of supervisory work.[12] The survey found that approximately 46 percent of a probation officer's time was spent in direct case supervision. Travel and record keeping accounted for 13 percent and 15 percent of that time, respectively; supervision and coordination of volunteers took up another 6 percent; and resource work and miscellaneous tasks accounted for the remaining 8 and 10 percent, respectively. These percentages tended to be the same in rural and in urban areas.

Surveys like the Texas study can be useful for any probation or parole department in planning and administering supervisory functions.

6. **Team Management of Probation and Parole Supervision:** The usual approach in probation and parole is to assign a caseload of specific offenders to each officer. The officer then provides direct supervision, employment counseling, referrals, and other services to each offender as required. Under this system, the probation or parole officer becomes a "jack of all trades"—or, as critics maintain, a "master of none." A variation on the standard approach, which attempts to deal with the foregoing criticism, is the team management concept.

   a. **Variations of the team concept:** There are several forms of team supervision in probation and parole. In many instances, basic caseload assignments are retained but members of a supervision team work together on case review and decision making. In other situations, task areas are separated, so that some officers specialize in the preparation of reports while others concentrate on providing services to the offender as counselors, resource brokers, or both.

   b. **Major advantage of team management:** Team supervision has the potential for providing more efficient services in probation and parole programs. Workers with special skills, talents, or interests in such areas as resource development, counseling of alcoholics or drug abusers, and job placement should be more effective in the team approach than in the traditional one-to-one system.

   c. **Community resources management team (CRMT) concept:** The community resources management team (or CRMT) concept was developed in 1975 under a federal grant from the National Institute of Corrections to the thirteen-state Western Interstate Commission for Higher Education. Today, the CRMT approach is being used by some nineteen probation agencies throughout the western United States (and presumably would work with parole as well as probation supervision).

      (1) **Basic elements of CRMT:** The basic structure of a community resources management team is a synthesis of four elements: team reorganization of staff; assessment of client needs; pooled caseloads; and resource brokerage.

         (a) **Team reorganization of staff:** The first step in organizing a CRMT is the reorganization of the probation staff into a unit consisting of a team manager, four probation officers, and one community worker. Each officer on the team concentrates on one particular area of probation supervision, such as alcohol or drug abuse, mental health, or job placement and vocational services. The officer need not be an expert in a particular specialty; but he or she must know what community programs and agencies exist to help a probationer solve that particular problem. The probationer, in turn, will meet not with the whole team but with the member best equipped to solve the difficulty faced at that particular time.

         (b) **Assessment of client needs:** Before a community resources management team approach can be formulated, an assessment of client needs in the department must be made. Each probation officer first prepares a profile on the needs of his or her clients. Next, all probationer-clients of the department are grouped on the basis of common problems (such as drug abuse, lack of education, and unemployment). Probationers are then assigned to teams that have been structured to handle their particular problems.

Once the CRMT approach has been adopted, each new probationer will be interviewed and his or her needs plotted on a needs-assessment form. The offender is then placed on a list or chart according to what is perceived to be the most serious need; and this placement will determine which team member works with the client first.

(c) **Pooled caseloads:** Under the CRMT approach, caseloads are pooled. The first officer to work with the probationer focuses on the client's most serious problem; but he or she simultaneously arranges appointments with other officers to handle lesser problems facing the client. As the client's needs shift, the case is reevaluated and the client is assigned to the team member best suited to handle his or her problems at that time. This pooling of caseloads is designed to provide more flexibility and creativity in solving the complicated problems faced by many probationers.

(d) **Resource brokerage:** The fourth element of the CRMT approach is the establishment of collaborative relationships with community agencies and other community resources. Unlike the traditional probation or parole model, in which each supervising officer deals individually with each service agency in the community, the community resources management team concept allows one team member to become the liaison with a particular agency—thereby fostering a more cooperative and productive relationship between the agency and the department.

(2) **Criticisms of CRMT approach:** Several criticisms have been leveled against the use of community resource management teams. Those most widely voiced concern the effects of team reorganization on the traditional one-to-one relationship between officer and client, the accountability of both staff and client, and the possible impact of CRMT organization on staff morale.

(a) **Effect on traditional one-to-one relationship:** One of the major changes in CRMT from the traditional probation or parole model involves abandonment of the exclusive relationship of one officer with a particular client. Officers may feel that this relationship is significant and beneficial, and may therefore be reluctant to release the personal hold they have on their clients.

(b) **Staff and client accountability:** Another controversy over CRMT involves the concept of pooled caseloads. Many departments fear that pooling will cause probation or parole officers to lose control over their clients and the ability to evaluate their own performances as well.

(c) **Impact on department morale:** Finally, critics claim that CRMT units are a threat to line officers in a department, because the same amount of work can be done by fewer staff members. This in turn is perceived as a source of friction and lowered morale within the department.

(3) **Proponents' rebuttal to criticisms:** Supporters of the CRMT concept are willing to focus on the same issues raised by its critics, but they see the management team approach as having quite different—and positive—effects in each of these areas.

(a) **Effect on one-to-one relationship**: CRMT advocates believe that the traditional one-to-one relationship is not weakened or abolished under a CRMT, but continues to exist between the client and an officer especially capable of dealing with his or her particular needs. In their view, the CRMT approach does not excuse team members from monitoring the client's progress but allows ample room for personal involvement between probation or parole officers and their clients.

(b) **Staff accountability**: Supporters of the community resources management team approach point out that staff accountability under this approach is actually greater than in the traditional model, because the former involves a better tracking system. The performance of probation or parole officers in CRMT's improves because each team member is accountable to and held responsible by other team members, and because members advise one another and share decisions. In effect, CRMT takes on the qualities of participatory management: Everyone on the team helps to fulfill department goals and objectives, and each team member contributes to the creation of an organization to meet those goals.

(c) **Client accountability**: Proponents of CRMT likewise contend that probationer-clients are more accountable under their system than under traditional approaches. Since the client works with a team rather than a single officer, his or her actions are observed by more people; and the chances of being caught if he or she violates the rules are correspondingly greater. During the first year of CRMT supervision in the state of Arizona, for example, probation and parole revocations more than doubled—which is consistent with greater client scrutiny and accountability.

(d) **Impact on organization and morale**: According to the National Advisory Commission on Criminal Justice Standards and Goals and many other experts, a fundamental restructuring or reorganizing of traditional methods of offender supervision is needed. The notion that a single officer should provide all services to an offender is seen as a narrow and obsolete view of the probation or parole function. Conversely, CRMT supporters see the team approach as allowing a probation or parole department to make the best use of the talents of its employees by relieving officers of much paperwork and the necessity of being "all things to all clients." Moreover, these proponents do not believe that the money-saving aspects of the CRMT approach are necessarily bad for morale, since good employees can handle more work more effectively and the emphasis may be on handling more cases rather than on cutting back on the number of staff employed.[13]

7. **Supervision of Juveniles**: The process for supervising juveniles on probation or parole is substantially the same as that for adults. Certain conditions of release—such as regular school attendance and obedience to parents or guardians—are unique to juvenile offenders; and casework counseling is likely to be more important for juveniles than for adults. By the same token, job placement and employment training tend to be of less concern with juvenile offenders than with adults.

8. **Supervision of Misdemeanants**: Unfortunately, very little supervision has been provided for these ostensibly "nonserious" adult offenders.[14] Some programs for misdemeanants released on probation have recently been established; but very few pre-sentence investigations are

made, and these offenders are infrequently referred to treatment programs. Where supervision does exist, it is common to find the assigned probation officers carrying excessively large caseloads.

9. **Interstate Compact Supervision:** In 1934, the U.S. Congress authorized agreements or compacts among the various states for "cooperative effort and mutual assistance in the prevention of crime." Since that time, each of the fifty states has signed an Interstate Compact for the Supervision of Parolees and Probationers. The Interstate Compact has been a very useful device for administering correctional services; and while the U.S. Supreme Court has yet to rule on the matter, its constitutionality has been upheld in state courts. The basic provisions of the compact are as follows:

    a. **Travel of offenders to other states:** Any state (the sending state) may allow a probationer or parolee to go to any other state (the receiving state) if "such person is in fact a resident of or has his family residing within the receiving state and can obtain employment there." Moreover, where the receiving state so permits, an offender may be allowed to enter its jurisdiction even if these residence and employment qualifications are not met.

    b. **Supervision in the receiving state:** Where such interstate travel occurs, the receiving state agrees to provide the same care and supervision for the probationer or parolee as its standards require for offenders released within that state.

    c. **Return of offenders:** If a sending state wishes to bring back a probationer or parolee who has been placed in another jurisdiction under the terms of the compact, officers of the sending state are empowered to apprehend the offender in the receiving state merely by establishing their authority and proving the identity of the person they want to return. The states have agreed to waive the legal requirements for extradition of fugitives in the case of such offenders; and a probationer or parolee who is released to another jurisdiction must sign a waiver of extradition as a condition of transfer to the receiving state.[15]

D. THE SURVEILLANCE FUNCTION IN PROBATION AND PAROLE

Once an offender is released on probation or parole, it is the job of the supervising officer to see that the client abides by the rules of his or her release.

1. **Underlying Problems in Complying with Conditions of Release:** Minor infractions or violations of the conditions of release may not automatically be cause for great concern on the part of the supervising officer. However, problems or instability in the offender's family, financial, or employment situation can lead to serious compliance difficulties and thus require careful scrutiny by the officer.

    a. **Deteriorating family situation:** A family situation in which discord, alcoholism, or other serious problems occur may require modification of the client's probation or parole plan. In some instances, the offender will need to be removed from the situation and placed in an alternative living arrangement.

    b. **Deteriorating financial or occupational situation:** When a client experiences significant occupational or financial difficulties, the supervising officer will need to investigate the situation to determine the problem and try to remedy it. If the offender loses his or her job, for example, the officer must seek to determine why. If the client wishes to change jobs, the officer must determine why and must then assess the suitability of the proposed new job.

2. **Basic Responses to Violation of Release Conditions**: If the supervising officer has reason to believe the client may have violated a condition of release, the officer investigates the situation to obtain the facts and then responds in a manner appropriate to the results of the investigation. In most cases, the response will involve one of two courses of action: increasing the level of supervision or initiating the process of revocation of probation or parole.

   a. **Increased supervision**: Where violations of the release terms are felt to be remediable, the supervising officer may decide, alone or with the advice of his or her superiors, to increase the amount and intensity of supervision over the released offender. Among other things, the client may be required to report to the officer more frequently or to begin intensive individual or group counseling programs. And in some instances, the officer may employ "jail therapy" (that is, short-term incarceration in a local jail) to impress upon the client the seriousness of his or her violations.

   b. **Revocation of probation or parole**: The officer's investigation may disclose serious, even criminal, violations of the release conditions. In this situation, the officer either advises his or her superiors to have the offender arrested and begin revocation procedures or (where he or she has the authority) personally makes the arrest and initiates revocation procedures.

E. REVOCATION OF PROBATION OR PAROLE

Revocation of probation or parole means incarceration for the offender in question. Compared to supervised release, revocation is more costly both personally and financially; and it is likely to be viewed as a sign of failure by the offender, his or her family, and the probation or parole officer. For these reasons, revocation is considered a very serious step, to be used sparingly and as a last resort. Since the procedures for revocation in probation and parole are somewhat different, the two areas are treated separately here.

1. **Revocation of Parole**

   a. **Historical revocation procedures**: Until fairly recent times, a parolee was deemed to have few if any rights in the revocation process. Only about half of the states granted hearings on parole revocation; and these hearings were considered a matter of grace rather than a right.

      (1) **Timing of hearing**: In states where hearings were allowed, the matter was often heard after the parolee had been returned to prison.

      (2) **Notice of charges**: Moreover, in several states where a hearing was provided, the charges on which revocation was being sought were not made known to the parolee until *after* the hearing had been held.

      (3) **Confrontation of accusers**: Finally, witnesses against the parolee in a revocation proceeding rarely appeared before the parole authority, even where the charges were

made known to and were disputed by the parolee. The usual practice was to rely on reports submitted by the parole staff and to keep such reports confidential.

Effect of procedures: The foregoing procedures obviously had a harsh impact on the parolees in question. In most cases, revocation was already an accomplished fact by the time a representative of the parole board visited the penal institution to review the matter and officially declare the parolee a violator. In a few cases, the board might cancel a warrant or field complaint and permit the prisoner to resume parole; but considerable damage frequently had been done by that point. The parolee usually would have been returned to the institution, seriously disrupting employment and family relationships; and he or she would then have to be released to begin the readjustment process once again.[16]

b. **Current revocation process:** The controversy over whether, or to what extent, a parolee had due-process rights in a revocation proceeding existed for many years. Some felt that if the granting of parole was an act of grace (and thus subject to withdrawal), then the parolee had no rights whatever and could be reincarcerated without notice or a hearing. Others argued that all the rights of an accused should apply in revocation proceedings, including the right to appointed counsel.[17] The debate persisted until the early 1970's, when the U.S. Supreme Court handed down two landmark decisions outlining due-process rights and current procedures for revocation of parole.

(1) *Morrissey* v. *Brewer*: In 1972, the Supreme Court in *Morrissey* v. *Brewer*[18] held that due-process rights—in the form of notice and a hearing—*did* apply to the revocation of parole. The Court ruled that while the state can subject a parolee to many restrictions that would not apply to other citizens, the loss of "liberty" inherent in parole revocation is covered by the Fourteenth Amendment to the Constitution and hence cannot occur without due process. Moreover, the Court found two stages at which the right to notice and a hearing apply: a preliminary hearing at the time of arrest and another hearing before final revocation of parole.

(a) **Rights at preliminary hearing:** At the time of arrest for a parole violation, the parolee is entitled to a preliminary hearing near the site of the alleged violation or offense to determine whether there is probable cause to revoke parole. This hearing is designed to protect the parolee from personal and financial damage should the alleged violation have no basis or support; and the parolee has the following rights at the hearing:

1) prior notice of the inquiry;

2) prior notice of the alleged offense;

3) right to appear in person;

4) right to present documents and witnesses;

5) right to a hearing before a neutral hearing officer; and

6) right to be given reasons for the determination made.

(b) **Rights at final revocation hearing:** Assuming that probable cause for revocation is found at the preliminary hearing, the parolee is entitled to a second and final hearing on the revocation issue. This hearing before the parole board must be held within a reasonable time after the parolee is taken into custody; and the parolee has the following rights therein:

1) written notice of the asserted parole violations and evidence in support thereof;

2) opportunity to be heard in person;

3) opportunity to present witnesses and documentary evidence;

4) right to confront and cross-examine adverse witnesses (unless the board specifically finds good cause for refusing confrontation);

5) right to a "neutral and detached" hearing body (that is, parole board or hearing examiner); and

6) a written statement of the evidence relied on and the reasons for revoking parole.

(2) *Gagnon* v. *Scarpelli*: The decision in *Morrissey* v. *Brewer* did not address the issue of whether a parolee was entitled to an attorney in revocation proceedings. One year later, however, the Supreme Court in *Gagnon* v. *Scarpelli*[19] held that there was a *limited* right to appointed counsel in revocation hearings, based upon the parolee's need therefor. This determination is to be made on a case-by-case basis at the sound discretion of the parole authority, taking into account whether cross-examination will be required, the legal and factual complexities of the case, the parolee's own skills and (most especially) whether the basis for revocation is the alleged commission of a new crime.

2. Revocation of Probation

a. **When probation may be revoked:** Probation can be revoked at any time during the period while the offender is on probation, on either of the following grounds:

(1) **New offense:** This would involve another criminal offense against the federal government, the state, or the local community.

(2) **"Technical" offense:** This occurs when the probationer violates a condition of his or her probation.

b. **Authority to revoke probation:** Only the court that originally sentenced the probationer and placed him or her on probation has the authority to revoke probation, unless the sentencing court officially transfers the case to another court.

c. **Evolution of due-process rights in probation revocation:** Due process in probation revocation proceedings was subject to much the same controversy as in parole revocation.

Four U.S. Supreme Court decisions illustrate the development of probationer rights to their current status.

(1) **Early view—*Escoe* v. *Zerbst***: In 1935, the Supreme Court in *Escoe* v. *Zerbst*[20] denied a claim that revocation of probation without notice or a hearing was unconstitutional.

(2) ***Mempa* v. *Rhay***: In 1957, however, the Supreme Court in *Mempa* v. *Rhay*[21] reversed its earlier position and held that due process requires a hearing before probation can be revoked. The Court also ruled that the probationer is entitled to adequate notice and to appointed counsel where sentencing is delayed until probation has been revoked.

(3) ***Morrissey* v. *Brewer***: As noted earlier, the 1972 Supreme Court decision in *Morrissey* v. *Brewer*[22] established due-process rights and mandated a two-hearing procedure for revocation of parole. Several jurisdictions subsequently adopted this model for *both* probation and parole revocation proceedings.

(4) **Current position—*Gagnon* v. *Scarpelli***: Finally, the Court in its 1973 decision in *Gagnon* v. *Scarpelli*[23] officially held that probationers are entitled to the same rights and procedures as parolees in revocation proceedings. Moreover, as discussed previously, the Court ruled that probationers and parolees had a right to appointed counsel where circumstances warranted.

NOTES

[1] Robert Shearer and James Moore, "Personality Dimensions of Felonious Probationers in Texas." Paper presented at the meeting of the American Society of Criminology, Dallas, November 1978.

[2] *Jones* v. *Commonwealth*, 185 Va. 335, 38 S.E. 2d 444 (1946).

[3] *Springer* v. *United States*, 148 F. 2d 411 (9th C. 1945).

[4] *People* v. *Dominguez*, 256 Cal. App. 2d 623, 64 Cal Rptr. 290 (1967).

[5] *Ex parte Heckman*, 90 Cal App. 700, 266 P. 585 (1928).

[6] National Advisory Commission on Criminal Justice Standards and Goals, *Corrections* (Washington, D.C.: U.S. Government Printing Office, 1973), p. 318.

[7] James Robinson *et al., The San Francisco Project*, Research Report No. 14 (Berkeley: University of California School of Criminology, 1969).

[8] Chamber of Commerce, *Marshalling Citizen Power to Modernize Corrections* (Washington, D.C.: Chamber of Commerce of the United States, 1972), p. 9.

[9] National Advisory Commission on Criminal Justice Standards and Goals, p. 318.

[10] *Ibid.*

[11] President's Commission on Law Enforcement and Administration of Justice, *The Challenge of Crime in a Free Society* (Washington, D.C.: U.S. Government Printing Office, 1967), p. 169.

[12] Texas Center for the Judiciary, State Bar of Texas, *Adult Probation and Community Corrections in Texas: A Master Plan*, Vol. 1 (Austin: State Bar of Texas, May 1977), p. 158.

[13] Charles McNamara, "Community Resources Management Approach Reports Success with New Team Concept," *American Journal of Corrections*, 39 (July-August 1977), pp. 32–36.

[14] National Advisory Commission on Criminal Justice Standards and Goals, pp. 404–05.

[15] Ralph C. Brandes, *Interstate Supervision of Parole*, "Probation," *Crime and Delinquency*, 14 (July 1968), pp. 255–60.

[16] National Advisory Commission on Criminal Justice Standards and Goals, pp. 404–05.

[17] *Ibid.*

[18] *Morrissey* v. *Brewer*, 408 U.S. 471, 92 S. Ct. 2593, 33 L. Ed. 2d 484 (1972).

[19] *Gagnon* v. *Scarpelli*, 411 U.S. 778, 93 S. Ct. 1756, 36 L. Ed. 2d 656 (1973).

[20] *Escoe* v. *Zerbst*, 295 U.S. 490, 55 S. Ct. 818, 79 L. Ed. 1566 (1935).

[21] *Mempa* v. *Rhay*, 389 U.S. 128, 88 S. Ct. 254, 19 L. Ed. 2d 336 (1967).

[22] *Morrissey* v. *Brewer*, 408 U.S. 471, 92 S. Ct. 2593, 33 L. Ed. 2d 484 (1972)

[23] *Gagnon* v. *Scarpelli*, 411 U.S. 778, 93 S. Ct. 1756, 36 L. Ed. 2d 656 (1973).

VII. MANAGEMENT OF COMMUNITY RESOURCES IN PROBATION AND PAROLE

In recent years there has been a move toward community-based corrections as an alternative to incarceration, sparked by disenchantment with prisons and a growing emphasis on reintegration of offenders into the community as opposed to treatment under the traditional "medical" model. These basic changes in the philosophy of programs dealing with offenders require a reappraisal of the roles of probation and parole officers in such programs. Voicing the opinion of many experts in the field, the National Advisory Commission for Correctional Standards and Goals recommends that probation and parole be oriented more toward managing community resources available to the offender.

A. "COMMUNITY RESOURCE MANAGER" ROLE

Unlike their predecessors—who were primarily counselors dispensing treatment—probation and parole officers acting as "community resource managers" have the responsibility of identifying the needs of their clients, coordinating those needs with available community services, and supervising the delivery of such services. Officers must marshal and coordinate the community resources available to educate and train offenders and provide them with housing, medical services, and other support; and probation or parole departments should have funds available to purchase a wide range of such services. To the extent that probation and parole officers are adequately prepared to function in a community-based system, they should be able to meet the needs of their clients more effectively and efficiently.[1]

B. TYPES OF COMMUNITY-BASED PROGRAMS AND RESOURCES: IN GENERAL

A wide variety of community-based correctional programs and services currently exist, ranging from programs linked to or operated by prisons through pretrial diversion or community service programs and resources available from the Veterans Administration (VA), the Law Enforcement Assistance Administration (LEAA), the Department of Human Services, the Department of Housing and Urban Development (HUD), and other federal or state agencies.[2] However, such programs and resources can usefully be grouped into eight basic categories.

C. INSTITUTION-RELATED COMMUNITY PROGRAMS

This type of community-based corrections involves programs that are adjuncts to penal institutions and are used as a method of "bridging the gap" between the institution and the community. The principal programs in this area—in which the inmate has an opportunity to try out socially acceptable roles in a planned transitional process—include work release, work furlough, family visits, educational release programs, and pre-release centers.

1. **Work Release:** Work release programs, which began to be used extensively in the 1950's, permit selected inmates to work for pay outside the institution, returning to the prison at night. The purpose is to help the prisoner eventually reenter the community at large, while serving the following specific ends:

a. **Provides for financial needs**: The inmate's earnings from employment on work release may be used to make restitution, pay debts, contribute to the support of dependents, or build a "nest egg" for eventual release.

b. **Serves as pre-release tool**: Employment on work release likewise provides a pre-release transitional experience in the form of increased levels of occupational skill and personal responsibility, and a chance to test new work skills in the community.

c. **Facilitates reintegration**: Work release can reduce the risks and fears of the offender and the community during the critical period of adjustment immediately after imprisonment.

   (1) **Provides stable role models**: Such programs give offenders the opportunity to associate with stable fellow workers and to gain acceptance on their own merits.

   (2) **Encourages community support**: At the same time, work release gives the community a chance to observe inmates in a normal employment setting and thus to better understand the offender and his or her needs.

2. **Work Furlough**: Before a prisoner is actually released into the community, he or she may also be allowed a "temporary pass" to look for a job to begin after release. Like work release programs, this helps the inmate to make a gradual reentry into the community and achieve a good start in life on the outside.

   Underlying merits of work furlough: The value of work furlough programs has been expressed by two commentators as follows: "Deep in the ethos of the United States is the normative value of work, historically at least. While the history for inmates is spotty and loaded with incredible inconsistencies, work furlough supports the work ethic with its emphasis on frugality, industriousness, and the determination to get ahead."[3]

3. **Family Visitation Programs**: Family visitation programs are another means of helping the offender reintegrate into society. Family visits are common in most prisons; but other services such as conjugal visits and counseling programs for inmates and their families may also be available.

   Certain family visitation programs likewise provide short-term furloughs for inmates. Such furloughs may be allowed for serious family emergencies, for medical services not provided at the institution, for job searches and—in the case of inmates who have demonstrated their stability—for additional time with their families during the period immediately prior to discharge.

4. **Educational Release**: Educational release programs are community-based in the sense that the inmate is enrolled in school while still incarcerated. In such programs, an inmate is permitted to attend classes at an academic or vocational institution in the community; and a plan for further education after release from prison is also made.

   In 1965, the Vocational Rehabilitation Act was amended to provide that offenders and ex-offenders who qualified were entitled to financial assistance for this type of program. The result has been a marked increase in vocational education for both offenders and ex-offenders.

5. **Pre-Release Centers:** This type of prison-related community program is discussed later in this chapter.

D. PRETRIAL DIVERSION PROGRAMS

Another common type of community-based program is pretrial diversion, which involves the placement of offenders in programs outside the criminal justice system *before* they are formally tried by a court.[4] The decision to divert an offender away from prosecution is made when conviction for the alleged crime is likely but the benefits to society from diversion are felt to outweigh the potential dangers of not prosecuting the offender. When supervision is a condition of the pretrial release program, probation officers often perform this service or arrange to have supervision provided.

1. **Benefits of Diversion Programs:** Advocates of pretrial diversion believe that such programs have certain advantages over other treatment methods.

   a. **Reduce stigma of conviction:** By taking the offender out of the usual criminal process before trial, diversion imposes no stigma of conviction on that individual. As a result, many of the obstacles to reintegration may be avoided.

   b. **Have economic advantages:** Diversion is also economical. The direct costs of a diversion program are substantially less than the expense of prosecuting the offender in a trial; and there are indirect savings in the form of employment of the offender and uninterrupted support of dependents.

   c. **Broaden scope of resources for treatment:** One of the greatest benefits of diversion is that it broadens the scope of resources that can be used to deal with offenders. Many offenders can be helped more effectively (and with a saving of time and money) through the variety of alternatives available under diversion programs.

   d. **Reduce caseloads:** A fourth argument for diversion is that it reduces caseloads in the courts while the rehabilitative benefits for the offender remain essentially the same.[5]

2. **Criticism of Diversion Programs:** On the other side, critics level the following charges at diversion programs:

   a. **"Widen the net":** It is alleged that some diversion programs improperly restrain and then "divert" arrestees who would have been released outright if the diversion program did not exist.

   b. **Tacitly admit failure:** Critics also charge that the principal arguments in support of diversion are essentially negative, in that they tacitly admit a failure of the criminal justice system by asserting that offenders are better served by being kept out of it.

   c. **Involve improper legal principle:** Finally, diversion programs have been criticized as being based on "unsound" legal principles. The argument is that if offenders are "innocent until proven guilty," no disposition altering their status (including diversion) should be made prior to a trial.

3. **Selection Criteria for Diversion Programs**: The success or failure of a diversion program is often linked to the criteria used in selecting those who may participate. Certain factors are positively related to an accused offender being diverted, while others work against selection for the program.

   a. **Age**: The younger the offender, the more likely he or she is to be selected for diversion rather than prosecuted.

   b. **Circumstances of offense**: Where the offense in question seems related to a problem (such as drug abuse, family difficulties, or unemployment) that might be remedied in a diversion program, the accused offender may be assigned to such a program. Conversely, those who commit violent crimes are not likely to be diverted.

   c. **Traits of offender**: If the accused exhibits mental or emotional problems or behavior patterns likely to be helped by a particular diversion program, he or she may be selected for that program. However, offenders who have a long history of criminal behavior or who otherwise appear to be poor candidates for reintegration will usually be prosecuted rather than diverted. In this regard, persons who have been through diversion programs without success are not likely to be selected in the future.

   d. **Deterrence considerations**: Finally, the deterrent objective may influence the selection of offenders for diversion. Where prosecution is felt to be necessary in order to discourage others from the illegal activity in question, diversion is unlikely even if the accused might otherwise appear to qualify.

4. **Types of Diversion Programs**: Diversion programs now serve a wide variety of adult and juvenile offenders. Many programs are concerned only with youthful and less serious offenders, while others are designed to treat accused felons as well as misdemeanants. Detoxification centers, drug abuse treatment, and numerous specialized programs exist as well.

   Example—Operation de Novo: The Operation de Novo diversion program began as a demonstration project in Minneapolis, Minnesota. Since August 1975, the program has operated under a contractual arrangement with the Hennepin County Probation Department and is set up to help juvenile and adult offenders of both sexes (only those accused of violent crimes being excluded). Individual counseling, group counseling sessions, and treatment of the special problems of youth, family living, and drug dependency are all part of the program. In addition, clients are offered opportunities for educational and vocational training; and other community agencies are called on to supply additional resources for the program.

E. HALFWAY HOUSES AND COMMUNITY TREATMENT CENTERS

Historically, a "halfway house" referred to a community-based facility operating as a transition or buffer to ease the reentry of prisoners into the community. The primary purpose of these traditional halfway houses was to provide residential and employment assistance. Today, however, halfway houses serve a number of purposes: They work not only with those released from prisons on parole, mandatory release, or at the expiration of their sentences but also with those still serving prison time but soon to be released and those granted probation in lieu of incarceration. Many halfway houses are designed to meet the special needs of drug abusers, alcoholics, and offenders with mental and emotional problems. Finally, the halfway house is being used to serve persons undergoing study or diagnostic tests, accused offenders released on bail, and neglected children in need of temporary placement.[6]

1. **Halfway Houses for Ex-Offenders**: As noted, halfway houses originally were used to aid newly released prisoners in adjusting to life in the community; and many still focus on this traditional service. Temporary shelter, food, clothing, and other assistance are extended during this difficult period. Typically, no specialized treatment is provided, the attention being given to meeting the basic physical needs of ex-offenders.

   Example: New Directions Club, Inc.: The New Directions Club, Inc., operates five halfway houses in the vicinity of Houston, Texas. Founded in 1970 by Sonny Wells, the club has a policy of staffing its houses entirely with ex-offenders and has a board of directors composed largely of ex-offenders. One of its five houses is for adult women ex-offenders, the other four are for men, and the houses together can serve about sixty clients at any given time. In addition to providing the essential services of shelter, board, and companionship, the New Directions Club helps with job development and placement, peer counseling, and referral services.

2. **Halfway Houses for Pre-Releasees**: In many instances, a prison or other correctional institution may operate (or contract for services with) halfway houses designed to accommodate inmates who will soon be released from prison. This arrangement permits inmates to receive the adjustment benefits that a halfway house can provide even before their sentences expire.

   Example—Federal community treatment centers: The Federal Bureau of Prisons operates several pre-release centers throughout the United States as part of its program to help reintegrate prisoners into their communities. These centers are designed to provide or obtain several types of services for selected inmates who are within three to four months of release from a federal penal institution. Offenders placed in these pre-release centers receive counseling, employment assistance, aid in furthering their education, and other assistance in their efforts to reestablish themselves in society. In communities that have no federal pre-release center, an effort is made to obtain the services of other public and private facilities to meet these same needs.

3. **Halfway Houses for Probationers**: A substantial number of halfway houses are designed to work with offenders who have been placed on probation. This type of center is commonly referred to as a "halfway in" house to distinguish it from houses that serve inmates released from prison.

   a. **Scope of persons served**: Halfway houses for probationers are intended for persons who are considered too great a risk for regular probation but who still do not require the more severe controls of incarceration. In some cases, an offender already on probation may be placed in a halfway house when he or she demonstrates adjustment problems that require attention but are not severe enough to warrant revocation of probation (with its attendant likelihood of incarceration).

   b. **Example—Portland House**: Portland House is a private, residential halfway house serving primarily adult probationers in the Minneapolis, Minnesota, area. One of several state and local community-based residential alternatives to incarceration in Minnesota, the program houses about sixteen offenders in what was once a fraternity house near the University of Minnesota. Members of the Board of Lutheran Social Services act as directors for the program, together with an advisory board composed of business, professional, and criminal justice representatives from the community. The house receives support from the Minnesota Department of Corrections, the Hennepin County Adult Probation Department, and Lutheran Social Services.

(1) **Services offered**: Portland House is intended to serve as an alternative to incarceration, and young adult felony offenders are referred here from the Hennepin County Probation Department and several other correctional agencies. Residents of the house receive personal, family, educational, employment, and financial counseling, and participate in group therapy five days a week. Some residents also attend Alcoholics Anonymous meetings; and all are expected to pay room, board, and restitution expenses and to support themselves and their families.

(2) **Staff members**: The staff of Portland House comprises both professionals and ex-offenders, all with a commitment to the program and its acceptance by the community. These staff members have been successful in achieving a low rate of recidivism among the probationers under their charge; and the acceptance of Portland House by the community is attributable to the staff's excellent public relations efforts (which include participation in neighborhood improvement projects and activities).

4. **Halfway Houses for Neglected and Delinquent Juveniles**: In recent years, halfway houses for juveniles (or "group homes," as they are frequently called) have been opened at an increasing rate. Some of these halfway houses serve neglected children; others work with those in need of special supervision; and still others serve delinquents.

a. **Need for juvenile houses**: In the past, neglected children or those in need of special supervision were commonly placed in detention centers, training schools, or even jail because no other facilities existed. In some instances, such children were for all intents and purposes incarcerated without having violated any criminal law. Public alarm at this practice has led to the establishment of separate programs for these juveniles.

b. **Example—Burnett-Bayland Home**: The Burnett-Bayland Home is located in the Houston, Texas, area and serves juveniles of both sexes between the ages of six and seventeen who have been referred by Harris County Child Welfare or the Harris County Juvenile Probation Department. These children may be abandoned or abused, physically handicapped or emotionally disturbed, or declared truant, runaway, or incorrigible by the court.

(1) **Services provided**: The services offered at Burnett-Bayland Home include shelter, food, clothing, medical treatment, education, religion, recreation, and sports. The home is located on eighty acres in southwest Houston and has twelve cottages, each housing a maximum of twelve girls or boys. Food is prepared in the kitchen of each cottage and eaten in its dining room; and clothing is provided free. Medical treatment includes a complete physical examination upon arrival at the home and attention as needed at a clinic located on the campus. Children at the home attend the local public school, and special programs are provided for those unable to attend. Nondenominational religious services are held every Sunday. In the area of recreation, the home has both a gymnasium and a swimming pool. Evening activity programs are scheduled while school is in session, with a more intensive program during the summer.

(2) **Placement at the home**: Individual families cannot refer children to the home, and the referring agency must have some type of legal custody of the child. Juveniles referred by Child Welfare are usually placed on a five-day emergency or a ten-day evaluation basis; and placement may become permanent after the ten-day period. ("Permanent" placements for these children average six months for those under twelve and eighteen months for those twelve or older.)

Children placed in the home by the Juvenile Probation Department are status offenders referred ,by the Youth Services Division of the department, who may stay for periods ranging from ten days to six months. This placement is voluntary, requiring written consent from both the child and the parents. After release, these children return to their homes or go to other voluntary placements.

(3) **Funding and resources**: Funds for Burnett-Bayland Home come from Harris County, with milk provided by the federal government. Local donations of clothing and limited financial assistance are provided by private citizens, service clubs, and other organizations for use in social and recreational activities. Harris County likewise makes Child Welfare and Probation Department resources (such as medical and dental care, counseling, psychiatric evaluation and therapy) available to the home.

5. **Halfway Houses for Special Problems**: Finally, halfway houses are being used more and more to treat persons with special kinds of problems. Typically, these facilities have a specific target population—such as alcoholics, drug abusers, those with psychiatric problems, the mentally retarded, and "runaways"—and are set up to deal with the problems of that particular population. Some of these centers are residential halfway houses, while others are limited to day care.

   a. **Example—Friendly House**: Typical of these halfway centers is Friendly House, a privately supported program in Los Angeles, California, designed to provide shelter for alcoholic women released from hospitals, jails, or prisons. Participants, who must come voluntarily and must absolutely abstain from alcohol, are expected to pay for their stay when able to do so; but no one is turned away or told to leave because of lack of funds.

      Friendly House has no professional psychiatric or social work staff, since its program centers around the principles of Alcoholics Anonymous. Residents help with cooking and other housework, and may come and go as they please (although they are expected to seek employment). Like a number of other halfway houses for alcoholics, Friendly House is independent of Alcoholics Anonymous but receives many contributions from members of that organization.

   b. **Example—Youth Shelter**: Youth Shelter is a halfway house in the Galveston, Texas, area designed to meet the needs of runaway youth between the ages of ten and eighteen. Young people upset with conditions in their homes and local communities frequently gravitate to coastal resort cities such as Galveston, where they soon find their financial assets and opportunities woefully inadequate. The Youth Shelter offers a refuge for these juveniles, and provides residential care and counseling to those who seek out the shelter on their own or are referred by agencies such as Child Welfare, Juvenile Probation, Texas Youth Council, or the Galveston Police Department.

      The Youth Shelter is one of many houses for runaways in a nationwide network of such facilities. The extent to which this type of service has grown can be seen in the development of professional organizations and workshops set up specifically to address the problems of runaway youth.

F. INTENSIVE INTERVENTION PROGRAMS

Another group of community-based correctional programs involves intensive intervention in the treatment of youthful offenders. There are two basic varieties of such programs: nonresidential intensive treatment (such as attendance centers or group interaction programs) and residential programs or out-of-home placement alternatives.

1. **Nonresidential Treatment**: Nonresidential treatment programs are designed to give offenders a maximum degree of freedom while providing an intensive delinquency- and crime-prevention environment. Placement in such programs often is the result of a court or parole board order requiring it as a condition of probation or parole. The most common types of nonresidential intensive treatment are attendance centers and guided group interaction programs.

    a. **Attendance centers**: Attendance or "day care" centers serve as an alternative to institutionalization for probation failures or for offenders who need more intensive care than probation but do not require incarceration. These programs allow juveniles to live at home while undergoing structured "in house" treatment that concentrates on education and counseling. Placement in attendance centers is by court order.

    b. **Guided group interaction programs**: Group interaction programs are primarily concerned with utilizing peer group dynamics to foster more socially acceptable behavior. To a large extent, these programs depend on the involvement of the youthful participants to accomplish their own rehabilitation. Such programs place the offender in frequent, intense group discussions concerning his or her problems and experiences and those of other group members. Group interaction treatment usually allows its members greater decision-making authority than traditional group therapy programs.

    Example—Provo Experiment: The Provo Experiment started in 1956 to help delinquents who were considered likely candidates for a reformatory. The program sought to apply sociological theory to the treatment of delinquents, using peer group interaction as its principal rehabilitation tool. Group decision making was permitted as a means of providing status and recognition for participation in the treatment process. The underlying assumption of the experiment was that delinquent characteristics are essentially learned and shared by the group and are therefore most effectively overcome by group interaction.[7]

2. **Residential Placement Programs**: Residential treatment in the intensive intervention area includes programs such as group homes and foster home care. This alternative is used when it is felt that rehabilitation would be difficult or impossible if the youthful offender were to remain in the same home situation.

    a. **Foster homes**: Foster home placement consists of putting the juvenile in an outside family setting on a temporary basis. The court does not administer such programs, but makes placement referrals to other public and private agencies. In many cases, families volunteer their services as homes for juveniles.

Foster homes vary according to the number of children they accept and the financial arrangements they have with the placement agency. In all instances, however, the idea is to provide a temporary family setting that is conducive to rehabilitation.

b. **Group homes:** Group homes differ from foster care in several ways. These programs are supervised by professional staff members of the responsible agency or clinic (who may also provide casework treatment); houseparents and other staff members are paid employees of the agency; and there is less "family" atmosphere than in a foster home.

Example—Meadowbriar Home for Girls: Meadowbriar Home for Girls is a Texas group home that provides full-time residential care and treatment for delinquents, pre-delinquents, and girls with mild emotional disturbances. Participants are referred for an indefinite length of time, with a minimum expected residence of six months. The guiding principle of the home is the importance of self-worth, self-reliance, and a positive self-image.

(1) **Progress classification system:** The stay of each resident at Meadowbriar Home is divided into four stages. Promotion through these progress units is based on the individual's growth, development, and general capacity for responsible behavior.

(a) **"TLC (tender loving care)":** During this initial stage, the staff aids the girl in developing socially oriented coping behaviors, external awareness, basic behavioral control, responsibility for herself and others, and physical self-awareness.

(b) **"ATT (attention)":** The second stage focuses on the development of self-awareness, "mental" self, socially acceptable attitudes, feelings, and values, and the internal resources necessary to solve the resident's personal problems.

(c) **"AMT (almost there)":** This third stage concentrates on the relationship of the girl with others and with her environment.

(d) **"HH (honor hall)":** The final stage tries to synthesize the resident's internal and external growth and awareness. Service to others is especially stressed in this last stage.

(2) **Scope of programs offered:** Meadowbriar offers many programs to its residents. The girls either attend school in the local school district or have special teachers at the home. Recreational activities include a wide variety of sports as well as yoga, modern dance, ballet, hair styling lessons, and field trips. Individual and group counseling is provided, and the home has a volunteer "big sister" program. Local churches offer Sunday night suppers; and volunteers from the community provide arts and crafts and drama programs for the residents.

(3) **Requirements for placement:** In order to enter Meadowbriar, a girl must be between the ages of thirteen and seventeen and a resident of Texas. She must be able to accept minimum levels of structure and authority and possess a reasonable degree of internalized self-control. A minimum academic performance level and motivation to participate in a school or work program is also required; and the home does not accept chronic runaways, habitual users of drugs or alcohol, serious offenders, the mentally retarded, or those with severe emotional disturbances.

G. HOME DETENTION

Too often, juveniles are detained when charged with the same offenses for which adults can be released on bail. Thus, a high priority is given to alternatives to incarceration of juvenile offenders. Foster and group homes are one answer; but a more desirable alternative where feasible is home detention, utilizing the supervision and consultation of parents. In places such as St. Louis, Missouri, where home detention has been emphasized, the results have been encouraging.

H. COMPREHENSIVE TREATMENT PROGRAMS

This type of program is distinguishable by the extensive scope of its services, facilities, and goals. Such programs may be publicly or privately administered, and may be either residential or nonresidential. Many are quite innovative; and all attempt to provide a positive experience as well as an alternative to incarceration for the offender.

1. **Example—Hope Center for Youth**: Hope Center for Youth is a nonprofit corporation in Houston, Texas, that operates residential programs for children between the ages of eight and seventeen. The center, which began operation in 1973, has both public and private funding and stresses a warm, empathetic environment and the need to treat each child as an individual. Structuring at Hope Center is based on small, personalized groups as a means of achieving the underlying goals; and the center attempts to work with the child's family wherever possible (to enhance the possibility of a successful return home in the future).

   a. **Requirements for residency**: Applicants for Hope Center must be residents of Texas whose intelligence level is dull normal or above (that is, the functionally retarded are not admitted). Applicants cannot be addicted to drugs or alcohol, and cannot be considered dangerous to themselves or others. Consent for placement at the center must be given by the applicant's parents or conservator, who will have primary responsibility for the relationship with the center.

   b. **Basic programs for residents**: Hope Center offers four types of programs for its residents:

   (1) **Wilderness Camp program**: The Wilderness Camp program offers long-term residential placement in a primitive setting for seriously disturbed youth between ten and sixteen years of age. Camps of nine children and two to three counselors are located in the forest land of East Texas; and the small-group process involves all members in decision making and the planning of group activities.

   (a) **Living arrangements**: Each group in the Wilderness Camp program lives in a campsite which the members plan, construct, and maintain themselves (with twenty-four-hour-a-day therapy). The children are removed from their anxiety-producing environments and find themselves in a relaxed but structured setting with a positive-oriented peer group culture. At the same time, each child maintains contact with his or her family and makes a four-day therapeutic visit to them each month.

   (b) **Benefits of camp approach**: The process of constructing their own living quarters, cooking their own meals, and maintaining their own clothes brings troubled youths face to face with the basic struggle of life—survival. Given the responsibility for life decisions and experiencing the consequences of those decisions, the children are in constant contact with reality; and informal therapy helps them to develop sensitivity to their own needs and those of others. Successful functioning in this group setting in turn forms the basis for structuring appropriate relationships with home, school, and community.

(c) **Ancillary services**: In order to ease the camper's return to his or her home environment, therapy is also provided to the child's family, and aftercare services are provided for six months following departure from the program. During the Wilderness Camp, the child's academic training continues through the Alternative School program (discussed below).

(2) **Urban Homes**: In contrast to the Wilderness Camp program, Urban Homes is a community-based program offering a range of small-group placements in foster or group homes for delinquent, predelinquent, and emotionally disturbed youths aged eight through seventeen. The average length of stay in the program is one year.

(a) **Foster care**: The Urban Homes program stresses therapeutic foster care to provide the child with appropriate skills, attitudes, and behavior patterns to live in a family context after treatment. The child is integrated into school and community life to the best of his or her interests and ability, while the foster family provides for his or her basic needs and offers a participatory family atmosphere.

(b) **Group home care**: Group homes in the Urban Homes program are organized on the same principles as foster homes. Six to ten youths live with a counselor in a family setting, and group involvement in maintaining the home is emphasized. Personal growth, positive relationships with peers, and success in school are basic goals for all groups.

(3) **Supervised apartment living**: This new adjunct to Hope Center was started to prepare older youth for independent living upon their return to the community. It is not a treatment device in the traditional sense, but emphasizes the development of living skills for residents who are at least sixteen and a half years of age.

(a) **Living arrangements**: Facilities for the supervised apartment program are two small apartment complexes near the center of Houston, with convenient access to bus lines, stores, and jobs. There is a staff–resident ratio of one to five, and the live-in counselors are available twenty-four hours a day. The average length of stay in the complex is six months.

(b) **Services provided**: As noted, the goal of this program is independent living, to be accomplished by simulating real-life conditions and teaching living skills. Residents are all involved in some combination of school, vocational training, and employment; and each must maintain his or her own apartment, do his or her own shopping and cooking, get along with roommates, learn to budget and save money, and make proper use of community resources. Attention is given by the counselors to crisis intervention and modification of improper behavior, with residents being taught ways to cope with behavior that could cause problems in keeping a job or living successfully on their own after leaving the program.

(4) **Alternative School program:** The fourth service offered by Hope Center is the Alternative School program, designed for youths who have been unable to cope academically or socially in public school. The school strives for an environment that makes students feel at ease—an atmosphere of acceptance, understanding, and assistance with personal problems.

   (a) **Structure of school:** The Alternative School has a student–teacher ratio of eight to one, which permits individualized programs and remedial work for participants. The goals for each participant are determined after a thorough assessment of his or her needs and aptitudes and a discussion with the student, his or her parents, and others who have worked with him or her.

   (b) **Scope of program:** The Alternative School strives to interrupt the student's past cycle of failure and to help him or her to become productive in school and society at large. Reality therapy is an integral part of this process, and is used to make the student realize that he or she is responsible for his or her own behavior. The participant is then shown that, with some effort, he or she can master subject matter realistically designed for him or her. Success in these efforts gives the child a sense of worth and recognition which serves as a base for eventual reentry into normal school life.

2. **Example—Florida Ocean Sciences Institute:** Florida Ocean Sciences Institute (FOSI) is a privately operated corrections program funded by the state of Florida, the premise of which is that natural resources can be used to stimulate productive behavior in juvenile offenders. (In Florida, this resource is the ocean; but similar methods could be adapted to mountains, rivers, the desert, or other environments.) The program currently exists in Tampa, Jacksonville, and other Florida cities.

   a. **Requirements for admission:** Participants in the FOSI Tampa program (which is typical) are boys from fifteen to eighteen years of age, usually referred by the Division of Youth Services. Most are on court-ordered probation, although some are under state supervision by parental consent. All participants must have at least average intelligence and a sixth-grade ability in reading and mathematics; and boys who have been involved repeatedly with drugs or assaultive behavior are not accepted. The prospective trainee is given educational and psychological examinations and a swimming test, which qualify him for a thirty-day trial period in the program if the results show a chance of success.

   b. **Basic elements of program:** The basic aim of FOSI is to modify behavior and teach proper work habits. When a boy is accepted into the program, he signs a contract that sets individual goals in basic educational subjects and in categories such as diving, seamanship, lifesaving, ocean science, first aid, electives (such as photography or marine maintenance), family relationships, and behavior. The program is nonresidential, with trainees living at home (or in foster or group homes).

   (1) Rules at the institute are purposely kept flexible and simple. However, two types of violations automatically result in dismissal from the program: assaultive or destructive behavior endangering others or the program, and use of drugs.

   (2) Incentives are used throughout the program to promote enthusiasm and maximum achievement. These range from sew-on patches and certificates to a cruise in the

Bahamas or Florida Keys, in which the trainees plan the trip, chart the course, cook, and maintain the engines.

c. **Success record of program**: FOSI maintains a five-year followup on former trainees, who periodically complete questionnaires. In its first four years of operation, FOSI enrolled 344 boys and has kept records on all but ten. A total of 279 boys went beyond the thirty-day training period, and 121 graduated from the program. Among these graduates, the institute reports a recidivism rate of 11.5 percent (representing crimes serious enough to warrant remand to the Florida Division of Youth Services, adult probation, or adult prison).

I. OFFENDER COMMUNITY-SERVICE PROGRAMS

In an offender community-service program, the convicted offender performs unpaid work in the community as a constructive, inexpensive alternative to short-term incarceration. Such programs —which reflect a growing emphasis on social as opposed to merely penal treatment of offenders—provide for greater diversity and "personalization" of sentences and offer the chance for more reciprocal involvement between the offender and the community.

1. **Origins of Alternative-Service Programs**: Community-service programs began as a result of several factors in the 1960's. Rising crime rates during this period, coupled with high recidivism rates, raised serious questions about the effectiveness of traditional methods of handling offenders. The costs of traditional incarceration (involving staff, services, and facilities) likewise continued to increase. Perhaps most important, however, was a concern for the social costs of incarceration, such as the weakening of the offender's family and community ties and the deleterious effects of prison life.

2. **Requisites of Community-Service Programs**: In general, penalties that provide for community service in lieu of prison should meet the following conditions:

   a. **Provide meaningful experience**: The task assigned should be one that is meaningful to the offender and beneficial to the community.

   b. **Promote personal adjustment**: The task should also aid the personal adjustment and development of the offender by promoting self-awareness and the acquisition of skills that the offender will be able to employ after expiration of the community-service penalty.

   c. **Promote sense of social responsibility**: Finally, the alternative service assigned should be one that makes the offender more aware of the needs of others.

3. **Administration of Programs**: Community-service programs are usually administered by the local probation department in conjunction with volunteer organizations in the community.

   a. Initially, the court must determine that community service is an appropriate disposition for the offender and enter an order to this effect, specifying the number of hours of service that must be performed. The offender is then referred to the community-service manager in the probation department.

b. The community-service manager consults with the offender and with various community agencies, which are advised of the offender's experience, education, interests, and abilities. On the basis of these discussions, the offender is given a choice of tasks and is then assigned to work with volunteers from the community. (For example, former Presidential advisor John Ehrlichman served a portion of his Watergate sentence doing community-service work with Indians in the state of New Mexico.)

4. **Contributions of Community-Service Programs:** Community-service programs can provide benefits for offenders, volunteer organizations, the criminal justice system, and the general public. Among the more significant advantages are the following:

   a. **Economy:** The original purpose of community service was to help check the rising costs of incarceration. Direct costs of maintaining the offender are curtailed by using existing agency personnel to operate the service programs (thereby avoiding expensive outlays for new facilities and staff); and indirect economic benefits are realized from the services provided by the offender to the community.

   b. **Reintegration:** Community service involves the offender in providing needed public services, thereby contributing to a more constructive and positive self-image. The offender may also develop skills or associations that will help him or her become established in an occupation after release.

   c. **Public services:** The general community may also obtain considerable benefit from alternative-service programs, over and above the reduced cost of treating the offender and future gains from his or her contributions when released. Certain public and charitable organizations, for example, would not be able to operate without help from such programs; and in other cases, an agency is able to increase its services as a result of offender contributions.

   d. **Protection of society:** Community-service programs also provide an opportunity for careful scouting of offenders on probation. Since probationers assigned to such programs work for agencies that supply detailed reports to their probation officers, the amount of time that the probationers are subject to supervision is greatly increased.

5. **Current Use of Programs:** To date, offender community service has been used somewhat sporadically in this country. Where it has been employed, however, the approach has enjoyed considerable success.

6. **Example—Alternative Community-Service Program:** The Alternative Community-Service Program was developed by Judge Richard L. Unis in Multnomah County, Oregon. The primary objective of the program (which began operation in December 1972) is to provide an alternative to incarceration for first offenders guilty of misdemeanors. On the theory that the community is the victim of crime, the service alternative gives the criminal an opportunity to make restitution to the community.

   a. Under the terms of the program, the offender—on a voluntary basis and with the approval of the sentencing court—agrees to work for a nonprofit organization for a period ranging from twenty to eighty hours. If he or she performs the assigned work in a satisfactory manner, the offender may be relieved of any further sentence.

b. By providing opportunities to serve the community, the Alternative Community-Service Program hopes to develop respect among offenders for the law, the courts, and social agencies. In addition, the program has the advantage of lightening caseloads for probation officers, reducing overcrowding of jails, and cutting costs for taxpayers.

J. RESTITUTION AND COMPENSATION OF VICTIMS

In recent years, increasing attention has been directed at the neglect of the victims of crime by the criminal justice system. Among other things, efforts have been made to provide counseling, legal advice, and financial aid to victims.

1. **Types of Programs:** Victim compensation programs usually require the offender to contribute to a state fund, against which the victims of crime may appeal to obtain financial aid. In victim restitution programs, on the other hand, the offender pays money from his or her employment earnings directly to the victim of his or her offense. Several states have developed programs of both types, with those in the states of Georgia, Colorado, and Minnesota being especially noteworthy.

2. **"Work Release" Programs:** In recent years, restitution programs in Minnesota, Louisiana, Kentucky, and Mississippi have been developed around a concept of "work release." The idea behind such programs is to maximize benefits to both the victim and the offender.

   Example—Mississippi Restitution Correctional Center: The Mississippi Restitution Correctional Center (MRCC), located in Pascagoula, Mississippi, was established in 1977 through the efforts of Commissioner of Corrections Allen Aults. Residents of MRCC are released daily to work at jobs in the community, returning to the facility at night; and they are not allowed to accept work paying less than a stipulated sum considered a fair wage by the center. MRCC thus offers several advantages: It permits offenders to avoid incarceration in the state penitentiary; it provides maximum benefits to victims from the wages earned by participants; and it helps to reduce the public cost of supervising and treating the participating offenders.

K. OTHER PROGRAMS AND RESOURCES

In addition to the various types of community-based programs previously discussed, probation or parole officers should be aware of other resources that may enhance their role as community resource managers. Among such additional programs and resources are the following:

1. **Veterans' Administration Services:** Many offender-clients are military veterans who qualify for VA benefits. Probation or parole officers should know how to help these clients obtain assistance, especially in the area of alcohol or drug-related problems.

2. **LEAA Services:** Similarly, the Law Enforcement Assistance Administration is a source of help to offenders and ex-offenders. LEAA funds have provided aid to community-based corrections in the areas of juvenile assistance, family crisis intervention services, and drug programs, among others.

3. **Miscellaneous Federal and State Programs:** Resources may also be available to probation and

parole departments from such federal agencies as the Department of Labor, the Department of Human Services, the National Institute of Mental Health, the Department of Housing and Urban Development, the Department of Agriculture, and the Office of Economic Opportunities. In addition, many state agencies provide welfare, individual and group counseling, and educational and vocational training to offenders and their families. The probation or parole officer should understand that a practical working knowledge of these resources—as manifested in, say, helping a needy client to obtain food stamps—is an essential part of his or her job.

NOTES

[1]National Advisory Commission on Criminal Justice Standards and Goals, *Corrections* (Washington, D.C.: U.S. Government Printing Office, 1973), pp. 322-23.

[2]*Ibid.*, pp. 232-36.

[3]Alvin Rudoff and T. C. Esselstyn, "Evaluating Work Furlough: A Follow-up," *Federal Probation* (June 1973), p. 50.

[4]National Advisory Commission on Criminal Justice Standards and Goals, pp. 83-85.

[5]*Ibid.*, pp. 74-77.

[6]John M. McCartt and Thomas J. Mangogna, "Overview of Issues Relating to Halfway Houses and Community Treatment Centers," *Guidelines and Standards for Halfway Houses and Community Treatment Centers* (Washington, D.C.: U.S. Government Printing Office, 1973), pp. 21-32.

[7]LaMar R. Empey and Jerome Rabow, "The Provo Experiment in Delinquency Rehabilitation," *American Sociological Review*, 26: 5 (October 1961), 684-85.

The author also wishes to acknowledge the helpful information contained in pamphlets and other materials supplied by the following:

Operation de Novo, Minneapolis, Minnesota

New Directions Club, Inc., Houston, Texas

Federal Community Treatment Centers, United States Bureau of Prisons

Portland House, Minneapolis, Minnesota

Burnett-Bayland Home, Houston, Texas

Friendly House, Los Angeles, California

Youth Shelter, Galveston, Texas

Meadowbriar Home for Girls, Houston, Texas

Hope Center for Youth, Houston, Texas

Florida Ocean Science Institute, Tampa, Florida

Alternative Community Service Program, Multnomah County, Oregon

Mississippi Restitution Center, Pascagoula, Mississippi

VIII. VOLUNTEER WORK IN PROBATION AND PAROLE

A. FUNCTIONS AND CHARACTERISTICS OF VOLUNTEERS: IN GENERAL

1. **Functions of Volunteers:** The term "volunteers" in probation and parole applies to all persons who provide services without pay to probationers or parolees. These services can take a variety of forms. Some may involve the supervision of released offenders (including companionship, advice, and support). Some may be direct services, such as podiatry, cosmetology, cosmetic surgery, or dentistry. And still others include such ancillary support as consulting, public relations work, or fundraising for probation and parole agencies.

2. **Characteristics of Volunteers:** Early volunteers in probation and parole were generally regarded as middle-class "bleeding hearts" and were often criticized for doing more harm than good. Today, volunteers are much more difficult to stereotype: They cut across all age, sex, race, and educational lines, and may include housewives, business people, truck drivers, attorneys, or psychologists. Many are retirees who devote a considerable number of hours each week to this work. As a group, volunteers tend to possess the basic personal qualities sought in professional staff members:

   a. Typically, the volunteer is a sensitive and concerned individual with maturity and control over his or her own life. The volunteer relates well to others and is usually a warm and caring person capable of giving and receiving love. The volunteer finds his work interesting and enjoys being of service to others in the community.

   b. Many volunteers also have prior experience that would qualify them to work as paid professionals; and a certain percentage find their volunteer work so rewarding that they do join probation or parole staffs.

B. HISTORICAL DEVELOPMENT OF VOLUNTEER WORK

1. **Origins of Volunteers in Probation:** As noted in Chapter II, the first volunteer work in probation—and the probationary method itself—is usually credited to John Augustus. Augustus, a Massachusetts bootmaker, visited a Boston municipal court in 1841, observed the trial of a man charged with drunkenness, talked to the offender, and then persuaded the court to release the man in his custody, on condition that the offender return to the court in three weeks. Augustus brought the offender to his home, persuaded him to sign a pledge to give up drinking, and helped him secure employment. At the end of three weeks the offender reappeared in court, where he was fined a small sum of money and released. John Augustus eventually gave up his bootmaking business to devote all his time to helping offenders. By the time of his death in 1859, he had worked with nearly 2,000 offenders on a voluntary basis.

   This early concept of voluntary supervision of probationers was adopted by several countries, which have come to rely almost exclusively on unpaid volunteers to provide such services.[1] (Japan, for example, has thousands of volunteers and only a few hundred paid probation officers.)[2] As discussed below, however, the use of volunteers in probation and parole systems in the United States has been subject to distinct cycles.

2. **Origins of Volunteers in Parole:** During the early stages of the present parole system, volunteer Prisoner's Aid Societies were formed to help released prisoners find employment and housing and meet other basic needs. In most early programs, parole supervisors were also volunteers;[3] and this situation obtained in the state of Texas until 1958.

3. **Decline in Use of Volunteers:** Following the early reliance on volunteer services in the United States, there was a movement away from the use of volunteers for supervision of released offenders. Volunteer programs require suitable people with the time and talent necessary for effective supervision; and many experts came to believe that supervision could be handled more reliably by full-time paid professionals.[4] Accordingly, statutes were passed authorizing payment of salaries to professional personnel, and volunteers turned their attention to other areas.

4. **Revival of "Volunteerism" in Probation and Parole:** After the movement toward paid supervisors in probation and parole, a swing back to volunteers began in the mid-twentieth century. Although exclusive reliance on volunteers is relatively rare, the number of volunteers used in conjunction with professional staff for probation and parole supervision has since increased dramatically.

   a. **Initial reinstitution of volunteer programs:** Juvenile courts (in Lawrence, Kansas, and Eugene, Oregon, for example) experimented with volunteers in the mid-1950's. Perhaps the most influential programs in this era, however, were those in Royal Oak, Michigan, and Boulder, Colorado.

      (1) **Royal Oak program:** A major step toward the renewed use of volunteers in probation and parole occurred when Keith J. Leenhouts became municipal court judge in Royal Oak, Michigan, in 1959. Since no money had been budgeted for probation services, Leenhouts assembled a small group of professional friends and sought their aid on a voluntary basis. These efforts grew into a strong volunteer program, which subsequently has been copied in hundreds of other communities.[5]

      (2) **Boulder program and conference:** In 1961, Judge Horace B. Holmes began using volunteers in programs connected with the Boulder, Colorado, Juvenile Court; and the first national conference of court volunteers was held in Boulder that same year. This conference stimulated the movement toward court volunteers by providing useful information for establishing and operating such programs.[6] In addition, the work of Ivan Scheier was (and continues to be) instrumental in spreading the Boulder experience throughout the rest of the country.[7]

   b. **Current use of volunteers:** By 1970, 600 volunteer programs in probation or parole had been established;[8] and these programs received a significant boost in 1973 when the Law Enforcement Assistance Administration began assisting them with federal funds.[9]

      (1) **Volunteers in probation:** Since 1975, there has been a remarkable increase in the number of volunteer probation workers. Volunteer programs now flourish in almost every type of community and court, particularly where the probation agency is strongly committed to rehabilitation.[10] The efforts of Judge Leenhouts in Michigan and the National Council on Crime and Delinquency have resulted in a nationwide organization called Volunteers in Probation (VIP), which publishes a quarterly newspaper on volunteer work in the criminal justice system.[11]

(2) **Volunteers in parole**: Volunteers are used less frequently with parolees than with probationers, but there has been a marked increase in this area as well. The American Bar Association, the Junior Chamber of Commerce, and other professional and civic groups have initiated volunteer parole programs, the most significant of which may be the National Volunteer Parole Aide Program (VPA) established by the American Bar Association in 1971. Since its commencement, the VPA program has enrolled numerous volunteer lawyers and parolees in more than twenty states.

(3) **Summary of current volunteer effort**: Table 8.1 illustrates the number of volunteer workers in probation and parole by type of position and level of government as of 1976.

c. **Reasons for revival of volunteer programs**

(1) **Excessive caseloads**: The most recent move toward volunteers in probation and parole probably began out of necessity, as a result of large caseloads and frequently unsuccessful supervisory efforts. It became apparent that volunteers could greatly increase the direct supervision of released offenders, since every hour spent in training the volunteer could be translated into fifteen hours with the client. The variety of skills and personalities represented among volunteers could augment the services provided by the system while relieving professionals of certain duties and permitting them to concentrate on those clients most in need of their time and expertise.

(2) **Inadequate finances**: Directly related to the problem of excessive caseloads as a stimulus to volunteer services, and perhaps underlying it, is the problem of inadequate financing of probation and parole programs. Many departments could not and still cannot afford to hire enough professionals for adequate service to their clientele. With the help of volunteers, however, more attention can be provided to released offenders who would otherwise be slighted. Thus, there may be weekly or biweekly contacts of an hour or more rather than the few hurried minutes that are all the professional officer alone would be able to provide.

C. ADVANTAGES AND DISADVANTAGES OF VOLUNTEER PROGRAMS

1. **Advantages**: Although the renewed interest in volunteers for probation and parole programs had an underlying economic cause (excessive caseloads and inadequate resources), several other contributions have emerged with the implementation of these programs.

   a. **Facilitate community involvement in probation and parole process**: By incorporating the services of concerned citizens, volunteer programs promote increased community involvement in probation and parole.

   b. **Enhance meaningful contact with clients**: Released offenders often are more comfortable with volunteers than with paid court staff, since they consider volunteers less threatening. In addition, the probationer or parolee may be impressed by the fact that volunteers provide their time and talents without pay. For both reasons, clients may "open up" more to volunteers and make possible a more meaningful exploration of their problems.

   (1) Because volunteers usually represent a more diverse set of personalities and back-

Table 8.1

Number of Probation and Parole Volunteers by Type of Position and Level of Government, September 1, 1976

Level of Government	Number of Volunteers by Type of Position									
	Total		Administrative		Counselors		Clerical		Other	
	Number	Percent	Number	Percent	Number	Percent	Number	Percent	Number	Percent
State–local total	20,263	100[1]	254	1	19,375	96	309	2	325	2
State	7,349	100	50	1	7,017	95	150	2	132	2
County	12,220	100[1]	201	2	11,678	96	148	1	193	2
Municipal	694	100	3	(Z)	680	98	11	2	–	–

– Represents zero.
Z Percent rounds to zero.
[1] Because of rounding, the percentages do not add to total.

Source: Bureau of the Census, National Criminal Justice Information and Statistics Service, *State and Local Probation and Parole Systems* (Washington, D.C.: U.S. Government Printing Office, 1978), p. 6.

grounds than professional staff officers, released offenders can more often be matched with supervisors who share their social interests and hobbies. Here again, a rapport between supervisor and client may be more effectively established when the two have interests and concerns in common.

c. **Broadened perspective for agency:** The diversity of backgrounds among volunteers likewise contributes a broader viewpoint to agency policy regarding the treatment of offenders.

d. **Provide potential employment and labor supply:** Finally, volunteer programs give the participants an opportunity to see if work with probationers and parolees interests them as a career. At the same time, volunteers are a "known quantity," with training and knowledge of the agency, and thus constitute a potential supply of competent employees.

2. **Disadvantages:** While the positive aspects of a volunteer program are considerable, certain problems may also exist (not all of which may be immediately foreseen).

a. **Cost of program:** Although a volunteer program may ultimately prove economical for the agency in question (in terms of reduced caseloads for paid staff and the like), it must be remembered that such programs still have a cost in money and staff time. Selection, training, and administration of volunteers takes at least some professional staff time away from the direct provision of probation and parole services.

b. **Inadequate service by volunteers:** Even with careful screening and training, some volunteers simply will not have the qualifications or commitment to render effective service to the agency and the offender. In certain instances, the individual's reasons for volunteering may be purely self-serving and may actually undermine the agency's goals and policies.

c. **Increased communication problems:** Additional persons involved in the treatment process create the potential for misunderstandings and conflicting strategies for supervision. This can result in a more complicated and problematic experience for all concerned.

D. OPERATION OF VOLUNTEER PROGRAMS

A considerable commitment of time and effort is needed to initiate, develop, and maintain an effective volunteer program. The key elements in this effort are recruiting, screening, training, and management. Weakness in any of these areas can seriously hamper or even destroy the program.

1. **Recruitment of Volunteers**

a. **Traditional techniques:** One very common method of recruiting volunteers has been through "word of mouth," with judges, probation or parole officers, and current volunteers alerting friends or acquaintances to the need for volunteers. Many successful probation and parole volunteer programs have been established in this manner.[12]

(1) Volunteers may also be obtained from churches, civic service organizations, and college classrooms. Colleges and universities are an especially important source of volunteers, since student recruits have the greatest potential for careers as professional workers.

(2) The foregoing recruitment approaches probably provide small volunteer programs with enough recruits for their purposes. Large programs, however, must sometimes advertise for volunteers through the media. Volunteers obtained in this way need to be more carefully screened than those referred by persons in the criminal justice system.

b. **Need for diversity in recruits:** One problem with all these recruiting methods is that they tend to draw volunteers most heavily from the middle class. This is not an insurmountable difficulty, since barriers between lower-class offenders and the volunteer can be reduced by close contact in the supervisory program. Nevertheless, a successful volunteer program should also attempt to recruit volunteers from minority groups, working and lower classes, and former offenders.

2. **Screening of Volunteers:** The organizers of most volunteer programs discover that finding people willing to volunteer is seldom a problem. However, recruiting must be done carefully in order to obtain genuinely committed and capable volunteers.

a. **Importance of screening:** As noted previously, not everyone should serve as a volunteer in a probation or parole program. When selecting persons to provide "one-to-one" help such as guidance and counseling, for example, recruiters should look for an individual who is especially mature, stable, motivated, and empathetic. And in all cases, a volunteer should be able to "reach out" and extend warmth, guidance, strength, and support to the offender.[13]

b. **Techniques of screening:** The screening of potential volunteers is frequently accomplished by analyzing information gathered from written applications and interviews. Volunteer registration forms normally contain questions concerning the applicant's occupation, hobbies and interests, previous volunteer work, and views on criminals and delinquents.[14] A sample application form is set out in Example 8.1. Upon completion of the registration form, applicants for volunteer positions are interviewed by agency personnel. These interviews permit a more direct and subjective evaluation of the applicant's motivation and personality.

c. **Need for high standards in recruitment:** It is important that the probation or parole staff responsible for volunteer recruitment maintain high standards and be willing to turn down persons who do not have the required qualifications. Strict standards are necessary if offenders and the public are to have proper confidence in volunteer services.

3. **Matching Volunteers and Released Offenders:** The information gathered in the screening process described above is also used to match volunteers with offenders. In general, assignments are made according to sex, personal characteristics, hobbies, and interests. Depending on whether the offender is deemed most in need of a role model or a close relationship with a peer, the client may be assigned an older volunteer or one who is approximately the same age.[15]

4. **Training of Volunteers:** Some agencies provide very little orientation and training for volunteer workers. In certain cases of "direct skill" volunteers (for example, a dentist providing dental work for released offenders), training may not be needed. Where volunteers are involved in supervisory tasks, however, training is important; and all volunteers require orientation to familiarize them with the probation or parole program and make them feel needed. Staff officers must also be trained to utilize volunteer services effectively.[16]

Example 8.1

VOLUNTEER APPLICATION FORM

All information provided on this form for the purpose of determining volunteer service for you will be held confidential. Your cooperation is appreciated.

NAME _____

HOME ADDRESS _____

HOME TELEPHONE _____ BUSINESS TELEPHONE _____

EMPLOYER _____

BUSINESS ADDRESS _____

OCCUPATION _____

SOCIAL SECURITY NO. _____ DRIVER'S LICENSE NO. _____

DATE OF BIRTH _____

MARITAL STATUS _____ SPOUSE _____

Are you presently enrolled as a student? _____ Where? _____

Education _____ Primary Interest _____

Do you drive a car with adequate insurance, and would you be willing to drive it to transport clients as part of your volunteer work?

Children; their ages:

Personal hobbies and interests:

How much time would you be able to give weekly?

What time of day would you normally be available?

Focus of special interest as a volunteer?

Volunteer service experience:

In what areas would you need preparation or training, and why?

By what name would you like your probationer to call you?

Have you ever been arrested? If so, please explain.

Have you ever been convicted of a criminal offense? If so, please explain.

How did you learn about this program?

Why do you want to be a volunteer?

Are there any personal things you would like to be considered in matching you with a probationer?

Please provide name, address, and telephone number for three personal references.

Having considered the opportunities and responsibilities involved, I hereby offer my services as a volunteer with the Adult Probation Department. I agree to complete the prescribed training, to work with the probationer assigned me for at least one year, seeing him or her in person at least once a week. I agree to hold all information directly concerning probationers in confidence, and to report to the supervising officer as directed. I also waive liability against _____ County in connection with my duties as a volunteer.

Signature _____

a. **Orientation function:** A training program introduces volunteers to the workings of the agency, and should give them a basic working knowledge of crime causality and the criminal justice process. Likewise, the program should familiarize volunteers with their responsibilities to the offender, the professional staff, and the agency. The volunteer should know how much time he or she is expected to spend with the client and the proper manner of reporting on meetings with the client.

b. **Specific preparation for services:** In addition to orienting volunteers to the probation or parole program and to their responsibilities therein, the training program should prepare them for the specific services they are expected to provide. In this respect, the program should make volunteers aware of resources in the agency and the community at large relating to their areas of service[17] and should prepare them to meet typical problems in those areas.

   (1) The training of a volunteer should help him or her relate directly to the offender and caution against "stereotyping" or "overstructuring" his or her response to clients. The volunteer must understand how the offender might see his or her problems, and be aware of the offender's motivations, capacities, and opportunities for change. By looking at the situation from the offender's viewpoint, the volunteer can reduce the adverse effects of having a background different from that of the client.

   (2) The training program should also emphasize the volunteer's role in helping the client to define goals and develop the necessary capacity to achieve them, and in arranging opportunities to meet those goals. Volunteers should help to instill a desire for change in their clients and help them to overcome any fear of change or new situations.[18]

c. **Training as a screening device:** Beyond its function of preparing the volunteer for service in the corrections process, the training program is another screening device to weed out persons who cannot contribute to the probation or parole process.

5. **Management of Volunteer Programs:** Volunteer programs can become embarrassing failures if not correctly administered. Proper organization and management require skill in handling the overall program and effective supervision of individual volunteers.

   a. **Management of overall program:** To an increasing extent, responsibility for managing the volunteer program in a probation or parole agency has been given to a paid professional variously referred to as "volunteer coordinator," "director of probation (parole) volunteer services," or "volunteer specialist."[19]

      (1) **Role of volunteer coordinator**

         (a) **Qualifications:** The staff member who serves as coordinator should have a background of solid experience in correctional work. Even more important, the coordinator must have strong administrative skills.

         (b) **Duties:** The volunteer coordinator must perform several important roles or functions in order to manage a volunteer program successfully.

1) **Program coordinator:** It is the task of the professional administrator to set up a functional division of work among volunteers, to delegate authority, and to define clearly the respective roles of volunteers and staff professionals. The coordinator must also be a liaison in establishing and maintaining relationships between volunteers and staff professionals.

2) **Program mediator:** The coordinator is the person to whom volunteers and paid professionals will turn when problems arise, complaints are lodged, or new ideas are presented in connection with volunteer services. In some instances, the coordinator will need to resolve disputes that may develop in the relationships among offenders, professionals, and volunteers.

3) **Policy maker:** The coordinator should have the major voice in establishing the policies and procedures that define the services provided by volunteers.

4) **Financial administrator:** The coordinator is likewise expected to direct (or at least play a leadership role in) the financial affairs of the volunteer program. It will be his or her responsibility to see that sources of funding are available and that the monies obtained are properly managed.

5) **Public relations:** A final and crucial role of the volunteer coordinator is to serve as public relations representative for the program. In this capacity, the coordinator seeks to secure public support and the various community resources needed by the probation and parole departments.

(2) **Common problems in managing volunteer programs:** In administering volunteer services, the volunteer coordinator often faces problems with professional staff members and with volunteer role expectations.

(a) **Staff preconceptions about volunteers:** One problem encountered in establishing and managing a volunteer program is the resistance of professional agency staff to such services.[20] This resistance tends to be based on certain myths or fears that have little basis in fact. Nevertheless, the volunteer coordinator must deal with such preconceptions realistically and forthrightly to ensure that they are overcome and that a proper working relationship is maintained between agency staff and volunteers.

1) **Unwanted competition:** Some staff members may fear that volunteers will "show them up" and that they will suffer as a result. The coordinator should help the staff professionals to see that the volunteers are not there to replace them or lessen their role but to supplement and enhance their contributions with complementary skills.

2) **Endangered professional status:** In a similar vein, agency employees may fear that volunteers will demonstrate that a college degree or other specialized training is not necessary for work in probation and parole, thereby undercutting the employees' struggle for professional status. Here also, the coordinator should point out that volunteer success in rehabilitating probationers and parolees has generally *added to* the perceived effectiveness of the paid staff through the pooling of skills and resources and more efficient use of available talent.

3) **Loss of paid professional jobs**: A related and common concern of professional staff members is that the use of volunteers will result in the loss of paid positions with the agency in question. The coordinator needs to demonstrate that this has not been the case in practice, and that volunteer programs can result in *more* paid personnel (for example, to manage and supervise the volunteers).

4) **Endangered relationships with clients**: In some cases, agency staff members fear that volunteers will endanger the relationships they have developed with clients and resent having to relinquish the satisfactions they derive from person-to-person contacts. However, the use of volunteers need not eliminate one-to-one relationships between the staff professional and offenders. The coordinator should explain that volunteer assistance gives the professional more time to develop relationships with the more difficult or interesting cases assigned to the agency and to seek out additional community resources for his or her clients.

5) **Unwanted scrutiny**: Staff employees likewise may resent scrutiny by "outsider" volunteers of their agency, bureaucracy, or procedures. It can be argued, of course, that agencies afraid of outside scrutiny may have serious deficiencies and lack the integrity to "clean house" on their own. In overcoming legitimate uneasiness with volunteers, the coordinator should point out that as volunteers become aware of the problems encountered in probation and parole work, they can become the best allies of the staff in obtaining better salaries, budgets, and working conditions.

6) **Inferior supervision service**: Finally, staff members may feel that volunteers— who purportedly lack the experience and professional training of paid personnel—will provide service of lesser quality, which ultimately will affect their own image and that of the agency. The coordinator must take pains to show that this has not been the case in practice, where the alleged differences in qualifications between volunteers and professionals have proved to be more myth than fact. Most volunteers are competent, well-qualified persons who can provide valuable services to the agency and its clients.

(b) **Conflicts in volunteer role expectations**: The volunteer coordinator must also eliminate conflicts in the perceived role of volunteers *vis-à-vis* their offender-clients and provide a consistent policy for the agency. There are two basic views on the extent to which volunteers working on a casework level are extensions of the probation or parole officer and should therefore exercise authority in relationships with their clients.[21] While arguments can be made for either position, both can be useful depending on the circumstances; and the approach selected should match the philosophy of the agency and the offender in question.

1) **Nonauthoritarian role**: According to one view, the volunteer in probation or parole should be a "friend" to the client while staff professionals assume the authoritarian role. The theory is that a volunteer perceived by the offender as a friend with strictly altruistic motives is more likely to be accepted as a model for behavior. Conversely, it is felt that if the volunteer is expected to act as an authority figure (for example, uncovering violations of probation

or parole conditions), a close relationship between the volunteer and the client may be difficult to achieve.

    2) **Authoritarian role:** The second approach takes the opposite view, that volunteers *should* assume an authoritarian role *vis-à-vis* their clients. The belief is that a relationship of authority makes it clear to the client that friendship with the volunteer cannot be manipulated—thereby increasing the respect in that relationship. Moreover, this approach sees the volunteer as an important source of information on violations of probation or parole, one whose reports may enable staff officers to prevent more serious violations in the future.

b. **Management of volunteers:** As noted previously, the second aspect of managing a volunteer program involves the direct supervision of volunteers. For the most part, the probation or parole officer is responsible for this supervision, which involves the following:

    (1) **Clarification of responsibilities:** The officer must help the volunteers understand that they have specific responsibilities to the professional staff and the agency, as well as to the probationer or parolee assigned to them.

    (2) **Checks on volunteers:** As part of the supervision process, the probation or parole officer must of course maintain checks on the volunteers working on his or her cases.

    (3) **Facilitation of proper communications:** Regular communications must be established between the probation or parole officer and the volunteers who are helping him or her. The officer should provide guidance and support to volunteers and otherwise take steps to ensure proper feedback.

    (4) **Removal of inadequate volunteers:** Finally, the probation or parole officer must seek to remove those volunteers whose commitment, effectiveness, or relationships with clients are below acceptable standards. This is rarely an easy or pleasant task, but it is essential to the proper functioning of the volunteer program.

c. **Use of monthly progress reports:** One effective means of checking on volunteer services is the monthly progress report submitted by the volunteer on each client assigned to him or her. The report allows the staff officer and the volunteer coordinator to review not only the progress of the released offender but also the type and quality of services being provided by the volunteer counselor. A typical monthly progress report form is set out in Example 8.2.

Example 8.2

VOLUNTEER PROBATION COUNSELOR'S MONTHLY PROGRESS REPORT

(Due on or before _____ of month)   Date:_____

Volunteer_____ Probationer_____ Officer_____

MEETINGS

Total number of meetings scheduled and kept: _____

Were any meetings missed? _____ If so, why, and how did you handle it?

Use of Meetings

(1) Discussion (Please check)
    (a) _____ Get acquainted   (c) _____ Problem oriented
    (b) _____ General discussion   (d) _____ Personal material
    (e) Other: _____

(2) Special Activities (Please explain)
    (a) Recreational

    (b) Home Visit

    (c) Other

(3) Emergencies: (Please explain)
    (a) _____ Probationer in jail
    (b) _____ Report violation of probation
    (c) _____ Family problems
    (d) _____ Personal problems

How was the emergency handled?

If the probation department was consulted, were you satisfied with the handling of the problem?

AGENCY CONTACTS

What community agencies, if any, did you contact for assistance?

Was satisfactory service obtained?

PROBLEMS IN THE RELATIONSHIP

(1) a. _____ No problems

    b. _____ A few minor problems

    c. _____ Major problems

        1. _____ Did not keep appointments

        2. _____ Attendance is irregular

        3. _____ Seems very aloof and distant

        4. _____ Poor attitude toward society

        5. _____ Does not accept advice

        6. _____ Does not follow through on things we talk about and plan

        7. _____ Does not seem to be forming a satisfactory relationship

GOALS

(1) What are the short-term goals you and your probationer are working toward?

(2) What long-range goals are you and your probationer working toward?

a. Progress to date has been:

_____ Minimal _____ About as expected _____ Good _____ Excellent

b. Progress since last monthly report:

_____ Minimal _____ About as expected _____ Good _____ Excellent

ADDITIONAL COMMENTS:

Do not write below this line

Comments from volunteer coordinator:

NOTES

[1]United Nations, Department of Social Affairs, *Probation and Related Measures* (Sales No.: 1951. IV. 2), E/CN/.5 230 New York, 1951), pp. 29–42.

[2] Rehabilitation Bureau, *Non-Institutional Treatment of Offenders in Japan* (Japan: Ministry of Justice, 1970), pp. 1–59.

[3] National Advisory Commission on Criminal Justice Standards and Goals, *Corrections* (Washington, D.C.: U.S. Government Printing Office, 1973), p. 391.

[4] Reed K. Clegg, *Probation and Parole: Principles and Practices* (Springfield, Ill.: Charles C Thomas, 1964), p. 10.

[5] Keith J. Leenhouts, "Royal Oak's Experience with Professionals and Volunteers in Probation," *Federal Probation*, 12 (December 1970), 14.

[6] Marie Buckley, *Breaking into Prison—A Citizen's Guide to Volunteer Action* (Boston: Beacon Press, 1974), p. 125.

[7] Ivan H. Scheier, Judith Lake Berry, Mary Cox, Ernest Shelley, Richard Simmons, and Dian Callaghan, *Guidelines and Standards for the Use of Volunteers in Correctional Programs* (Washington, D.C.: U.S. Government Printing Office, 1972).

[8] James D. Jorgensen and Ivan H. Scheier, *Volunteer Training for Courts and Corrections* (Metuchen, N.J.: Scarecrow Press, 1973), p. viii.

[9] Gary M. Holland, "A Small County's Answer to Community-Based Programs," *Juvenile Justice*, 26 (May 1975), 21–26.

[10] Ivan H. Scheier, "The Professional and the Volunteer in Probation: Perspectives on an Emerging Relationship," *Federal Probation*, 6 (June 1970), 12–18.

[11] Buckley, pp. 125–26.

[12] *Volunteer Programs in Courts; Collected Papers on Productive Programs* (Washington, D.C.: Office of Juvenile Delinquency and Youth Development, 1969), p. 61.

[13] Scheier *et al.*

[14] *Volunteer Programs in Courts*, pp. 81–82.

[15] *Ibid.*, p. 62.

[16] Scheier, pp. 12–18.

[17] Jorgensen and Scheier, p. 12.

[18] Charles Horejsi, "Training for the Direct-Service Volunteer in Probation," *Federal Probation*, 37 (September 1973), 38–41.

[19] Scheier *et al.*

[20] *Ibid.*, p. 41.

[21] Clegg, p. 147

IX. CURRENT AND EMERGING TRENDS
   IN PROBATION AND PAROLE

Probation and parole have received considerable attention from lawmakers, the press, and the general public in recent years. Some contend that these programs (especially parole) have been failures, while others see them as scapegoats of the rehabilitative ideal which have never been properly utilized. Whatever the case, the theoretical assumptions underlying probation and parole are being challenged; and programs are being modified and even eliminated in some instances. Given the fluidity of the area, it may be helpful in this final chapter to note various changes now occurring or likely to occur in the future.

A. RESTRICTIONS ON FORECASTING

At the outset, one should keep in mind the limitations on forecasting the future course of events in probation and parole or any other field. Events presently unforeseen could have a profound impact on corrections, especially since probation and parole interrelate with other aspects of the criminal justice system. A decision to eliminate parole, for example, could have the immediate effect of "backing up" prison populations—which could lead in turn to greater numbers of offenders being placed on probation. And, of course, broad political and social factors can affect the entire criminal justice system—including probation and parole. Throughout the following discussion of trends, these inherent limitations of forecasting should be borne in mind.

B. CURRENT ISSUES AND TRENDS

To a considerable extent, the current issues and trends in probation and parole reflect changing philosophies in the corrections area. In particular, attention is being focused on sentencing laws, the extent to which probation should be granted, and such parole issues as parole board composition, hearing procedures, decision-making criteria, and the viability of parole in the criminal justice system.

1. **Correctional Philosophy:** Perhaps the most significant current trends are in the area of correctional philosophy.

    a. Until recently, assumptions on how society should deal with offenders were dominated by the "Positive School" and the humanitarian movements of the nineteenth century. Reform efforts were largely devoted to improving policies and programs, rather than challenging their theoretical assumptions; societal responses emphasizing retribution and deterrence tended to be minimized; and rehabilitation and prevention as correctional goals were enthusiastically endorsed.

    b. Today, however, public concern over crime has led to a fundamental reconsideration of these approaches. Acts of violence by offenders released on probation or parole are being censured, and virtually all segments of society are demanding accountability and a reassessment of the correctional process.

2. **Sentencing Laws:** One indication of the shift in correctional philosophy is the current trend away from indeterminate sentences and back to the definite sentence.

   a. **Origins of the definite sentence:** The fixed or definite sentence has its theoretical basis in the "Classical School" of criminology that arose during the eighteenth century. As discussed in Chapter I, this philosophy considered criminal behavior a rational, free-will choice by the criminal and advocated punishment according to the crime committed. Pursuant to this goal of "making the punishment fit the crime," each offense had a set penalty (such as incarceration in prison for a fixed period of time).

   b. **Origins of indeterminate sentence:** The concept of indeterminate sentences developed from the "Positive School" of criminology and humanitarian movements in the nineteenth century. Essentially, Positivist philosophy rejected the free-will theory of crime in favor of determinism, which assumed that crime was primarily the result of factors over which the criminal had little or no control. This assumption, together with the Positivist faith in scientific observation and research, fostered the belief that the factors responsible for criminal behavior could be identified and changed; and the emphasis in corrections shifted to a rehabilitative approach aimed at treating the criminal rather than the crime.

   A natural corollary of the rehabilitation approach was to substitute indeterminate sentences for the definite sentences adopted under the Classical School. Since criminal behavior was viewed as a "disease," such sentences gave the corrections process sufficient time to find and apply the proper cure in each case.[1]

   c. **Present trend away from indeterminate sentence:** As noted, there is now a movement away from the indeterminate sentence (which has prevailed for decades in this country). Penologists have begun to doubt their ability to reform or rehabilitate, at least in a prison setting; and crime rates have remained high despite larger prison populations and increasing costs of correction. For these and other reasons, there is a growing trend to return to fixed sentences, whereby a person who commits a particular crime receives a specific punishment set for that offense.[2] States that have adopted or are considering determinate-sentence laws include Alaska, California, Colorado, Connecticut, Florida, Illinois, Indiana, Maine, Minnesota, Ohio, South Dakota, Virginia, and Washington.

   Example: Changes in the Illinois corrections procedure in the wake of a return to determinate sentencing are indicative of this movement. The Pardon and Parole Board in that state has been eliminated in favor of a Prisoner Review Board to oversee rules concerning "good time" and the supervision of prisoners who wish to continue under the former indeterminate-sentence system. A period of mandatory supervision now follows release under the new system, with a period of post-release scrutiny shorter than former periods of parole (since the prisoner has been supervised during his or her determinate sentence).

3. **Probation:** In comparison with sentencing procedures or parole (discussed below), where fundamental changes are being proposed or implemented, probation seems well-established in this country. However, there is concern over the policy of some courts to grant probation simply because of a perceived failure of the prison system to rehabilitate offenders. Indiscriminate use of probation may "skew" data such as recidivism rates among probationers and may undermine public confidence in the probation process (which, like other parts of the criminal justice system, is ultimately held accountable for its ability to protect the public).

4. **Parole:** At the present time, traditional parole concepts and procedures are being challenged by a spectrum of critics encompassing prison inmates, academicians, politicians, the press, and the general public. Theoretical assumptions, parole board composition, and decision-making procedures are all under attack;[3] and some states have abolished parole in favor of mandatory-release procedures.

a. **Challenges to parole theory:** Perhaps the most important criticism of parole concerns its basic premise that inmates should be released from prison at a time when their release would entail the least risk to society and when rehabilitation of the offender is most likely to occur. This principle requires that the timing of release be flexible and discretionary; and it assumes that the optimum time for release can be ascertained by the releasing agency. Both of these latter points have come under increasing attack in recent years.

(1) **Discretionary power of parole authority:** Parole boards typically are free to grant or withhold parole subject only to the broadest statutory guidelines. The board is not bound to follow any objective criteria (such as prediction devices based on empirical research); and while it may consider the offender's past history, adjustment to institutional treatment programs, and plans, the members are free to reach their decision in any manner they choose. Such wide discretion has been the source of severe criticism, especially from prisoners themselves.[4]

(a) **Effect on inmates:** In the absence of clearly defined decision-making criteria, prison inmates may come to believe that there is a subjective but unpredictable "magic formula" for parole consideration. This belief is reinforced when they observe certain inmates being released while others guilty of similar offenses and having similar institutional records are denied parole. Such uncertainty produces frustration, bitterness, and a cynical attitude that prisoners must "con" the parole board into granting them parole.

(b) **Effect on credibility of decisions:** The discretionary nature of parole decisions also makes them suspect among observers of the process. If nothing else, the paroling authority is left vulnerable to charges of abuse of power and accusations that its decisions are based on political, economic, and institutional considerations rather than the goals of rehabilitating offenders and protecting the public.[5]

(2) **Ability to determine proper time for release:** The second major criticism of parole theory attacks the assumption that the paroling authority can determine the time when release offers the greatest chance for rehabilitation and the least risk to society. This assumption has been challenged on the ground that such an "optimum" time may be impossible to ascertain and may not even exist in some cases. Some critics contend that an "optimum" time is irrelevant because no person can accurately predict the future behavior of another. Such attacks go to the heart of the parole concept.

b. **Composition of parole boards:** Parole boards themselves have been criticized for the way in which their members are selected. In nearly all states, board members are appointed; and while some jurisdictions require that appointees meet certain standards of education or experience, many states have no eligibility requirements whatever. Critics therefore charge that boards are vulnerable to (if not dominated by) purely political considerations which have no place in the parole system.

c. **Parole hearing procedures**: The procedures used in deciding on parole have also been attacked. While these procedures vary from jurisdiction to jurisdiction, the following characteristics are most frequently criticized:

(1) **Secret hearings**: Parole board proceedings are usually conducted in secret, and are never open to the general public.

(2) **Inmate attendance at hearings**: Most boards allow inmates to be present at their parole hearings, but this right is not universally recognized. And even where the inmate attends a hearing, some states permit him or her to meet with only one board member and others do not permit a meeting with any of the final decision makers.[6]

(3) **No representation by counsel**: In most states, inmates being considered for parole are not entitled to be represented by counsel or to have others speak on their behalf except by express consent of the board. (Some boards will receive written opinions and evidence from friends and relatives of the offender and opinions from law-enforcement agencies or others prior to making their decisions.[7])

(4) **Written record of the proceedings**: Less than half the states require the parole board to maintain a formal, written transcript of parole hearings. Since there is no formal appeal of parole decisions in the courts and no requirement that a decision be explained to the inmate, it may be felt that formal records are unnecessary.

(5) **Overall absence of procedural due process**: The foregoing characteristics of parole hearings underscore the absence of due process and the conception of parole as an administrative rather than judicial function. The prisoner has few rights in the parole decision process beyond those granted by the legislature or the parole board itself.[8]

d. **Criteria for parole decisions**: Finally, certain factors implicitly relied on in making parole decisions have come under increasing criticism. In particular, criteria that emphasize personality change, criminal record, level of involvement with institutional programs, and institutional adjustment have been challenged as being inadequate or invalid bases for parole decision making.

(1) **Personality change**: It is generally agreed that a change in personality *may* indicate rehabilitation. However, critics assert that such "changes" may be nothing more than a manipulative effort to obtain release, and that parole boards cannot accurately distinguish between real and feigned behavior patterns.

(2) **Criminal record**: The past criminal record of an inmate being considered for parole may be used by the board to diagnose the habitual criminal and deal with him or her accordingly. However, problems arise with respect to offenders who have committed a relatively serious crime but have no prior record. For example, the person who commits a murder in a fit of passion is unlikely to encounter a similar set of circumstances in the future and may therefore be a rather safe risk for parole;[9] but the nature of his or her single crime may evoke such a strong negative response that parole is unlikely.

(3) **Involvement in institutional programs**: It is often assumed that a prisoner's involvement in institutional programs will bring about the desired goal of rehabilitation. Critics point out two important problems with this criterion.

(a) **Improper motivation:** First, inmates may participate in various programs only because they believe that the parole board wants them to do so. This is a reflection of the "guessing game" atmosphere generated by discretionary decision making (discussed earlier), and affords little probative evidence about an inmate's progress toward rehabilitation.

(b) **Problems with programs:** Second, even when inmates conscientiously participate in prison programs, the programs may be erratically administered. For example, it is not uncommon for an inmate's "suggested program" to be shifted and rearranged constantly, producing frustration for the inmate and giving no real indication of his or her progress toward rehabilitation or lack thereof.

(4) **Adjustment to institution:** Parole boards often give considerable weight to evidence that an inmate has adjusted successfully to prison life. However, critics question whether a prisoner who adjusts well to incarceration is necessarily better prepared for life in the outside world, since his or her adjustment could also signify a childlike dependency on the ordered prison routine or mere "game playing" to secure release.

e. **The future of parole:** Despite the breadth and seriousness of the attacks on existing parole concepts and procedures, most jurisdictions still believe that parole serves a useful purpose. States such as Texas, for example, are expanding their parole organizations; and even critics of the present system may view the total elimination of parole as "throwing the baby out with the bathwater." As one commentator has written: "To those who say 'let's abolish parole,' I say that as long as we use imprisonment in this country, we will have to have someone, somewhere with the authority to release people from imprisonment. Call it parole—call it what you will, it's one of those jobs that has to be done."[10]

(1) **Continuing need for supervision:** Among other things, offenders who leave prison—whether on parole or by discharge at the conclusion of their sentences—generally require some period of supervision and guidance. Whatever the techniques used to determine the inmate's date of release (that is, whether parole is available or not), the transition from incarceration to the community requires assistance.[11]

(2) **Likelihood of changes in parole systems:** At the same time, however, much of the criticism directed at existing parole systems has merit and suggests that changes are likely to occur. For example, due-process standards will probably be formulated for parole hearings; and parole boards may be required to establish and follow clearly articulated criteria for parole decision making.

C. EMERGING TRENDS

In addition to the issues discussed in the previous section, a number of emerging trends may have a long-range impact on probation, parole, and community-based corrections. The most important of these trends appear to be demographic and procedural changes, the accreditation movement, and social and cultural shifts.

1. **Demographic Changes:** United States census data and other sources indicate shifts in population size, composition, and mobility for this country in the years ahead. For example, such data show that the American population is continuing to increase, but at a decreasing

rate attributable to factors such as delayed marriages, birth control, and legalized abortion. These demographic shifts in turn may cause changes in the clientele and staff for corrections programs.

a. **Changes in clientele:** On the basis of present knowledge of offender characteristics and population trends, it seems likely that most offenders will continue to be young people. The increasing percentage of minorities in society and the increasing number of female offenders suggest that a larger percentage of offenders will be women and minority group members. Rehabilitation programs and other corrections efforts will need to take account of and plan for these compositional changes.

b. **Changes in staff:** Changes in the composition, education, and professionalization of probation and parole staffs can also be expected in the future. As a result of well-established social movements, laws, and recruiting policies, women and minority group members are likely to constitute a greater percentage of corrections staffs; and the use of volunteers and paraprofessionals can also be expected to increase. An upgrading of employment criteria and the establishment of criminal justice education and training programs are encouraging the professionalization of probation and parole staffs; and the consolidation of probation and parole services into statewide systems should serve as a further impetus to professionalization.[12]

2. **Changes in Professional Roles:** In addition to the compositional changes just discussed, trends in the areas of counselor-coordinator functions and law-enforcement responsibilities may involve changes in the professional roles of probation and parole staff members.

a. **"Counselor" role vs. community resource coordination:** As discussed earlier in the text, the counseling function in probation and parole is likely to assume less importance as the role of the staff member as community resource coordinator increases. Reflecting this change in function, professional education and training of staff members can be expected to place primary emphasis on finding and implementing community services and resources.[13]

b. **Possible transfer of surveillance function to police:** It has been argued that transfer of the surveillance functions of probation and parole to law-enforcement agencies would promote the image of probation and parole as supportive rather than restrictive in nature. Proponents of such a transfer assert that law-enforcement agencies are also better equipped to deal with surveillance and that this responsibility is rightfully theirs. At present, however, opinions on this issue still vary widely.

3. **Procedural Changes:** Probation and parole have traditionally been considered privileges granted *ex gratia* by the criminal justice system, so that due-process safeguards for the offender were not required. As noted in Chapter VI, however, this position has been changed by Supreme Court decisions with respect to probation or parole revocation; and many have insisted that due-process rights should apply to parole decision making as well.[14] Among other things, it is argued that inmates should have the right to appear in person and to be represented by counsel at hearings, the right to review their files, and the right to an explanation of and an opportunity to appeal the decision of the paroling authority. Similar reforms have been proposed for probation.

4. **New Programs:** The following programs in probation and parole, inaugurated in recent years, should be more widely adopted in the future:

a. **Shock probation**: In October 1965, the state of Ohio adopted a "shock probation" law.[15] Based on the idea that it is the shock of incarceration rather than the length of time served that has therapeutic and deterrent value, the Ohio law provides that, under certain stipulated conditions, an offender sentenced to prison can apply for suspension of sentence after having served one month's time. The court must act on this petition within a specified time, and may also grant an early release on its own initiative.

   (1) "Shock probation" has also been adopted in Idaho, Indiana, Kentucky, and Texas. Other states (such as Maine and North Carolina) utilize "split-sentencing" probation, which likewise involves a period of incarceration followed by probation.

   (2) After its success with shock probation, Ohio enacted a corollary "shock parole" law, which specifies that an inmate who meets certain criteria may be given parole after serving six months of his or her sentence. The conditions for shock parole relate to the nature of the inmate's offense and the perceived risk to the community from his or her release on parole.[16]

b. **Mutual Agreement Programming (MAP)**: A number of states have begun using Mutual Agreement Programming (MAP) in place of traditional parole decision making. The MAP procedure involves a legally enforceable written contract among the inmate, representatives of the penal institution, and the parole agency. The contract reflects a plan for the offender to achieve specified goals in areas such as education, training, counseling, and behavior in prison. The institution agrees to provide its available resources in furtherance of these goals, and an independent party is called on to determine whether or not the terms of the contract have been fulfilled. If they have, a target date established in the contract becomes the inmate's parole release date.

   Although the MAP approach has strong supporters, others feel that it is overly idealistic and could result in the premature release of dangerous offenders.

c. **Graduated release**: Another suggested method for releasing offenders attempts to deal with the problem of predicting an optimum date for release (discussed previously). This system would take inmates through graduated stages of release, each involving a relatively greater degree of freedom. Examples of this approach include work-release, furlough, and various community-corrections programs.

   Advantages of graduated-release concept: Graduated-release programs have distinct advantages. By gradually lessening the restrictions on inmates, it is possible to observe their behavior and assess their capability for a safe return to society over a period of time. Those who continue to exhibit unacceptable behavior can be given further institutionalization or some alternative treatment. At the same time, government (at the local, state, or federal level) can assist the convict in reintegration, even though its primary concern is protection of society. This furthers both the surveillance and rehabilitation goals of parole, since the readjustments of the offender at each stage of release make it less likely that he or she will return to a life of crime when ultimately discharged.

d. **Community-based corrections**: For several reasons, community-based correctional programs—including probation, pretrial diversion, foster and group homes, community treatment centers, and volunteer and paraprofessional programs—may be expected to continue. Chief among these reasons is a pervasive doubt about the effectiveness of large, isolated prisons in rehabilitating or even controlling offenders. To a large extent, therefore, community custody and community or regional corrections centers will supplement the construction of traditional central prisons.

At the same time, it must be acknowledged that the atmosphere in some community and regional centers is not noticeably better than that of the traditional prisons, detention centers, and jails they are designed to replace. Proper funding and planning will be required if such programs are to meet their stated goals.

5. **"Management by Objectives"**: A welcome trend in probation and parole is the increased adoption of modern managerial techniques, such as Management by Objectives (MBO).[17] First used by corporate business, MBO is now being employed in numerous organizational settings, including all phases of probation and parole.

   a. **MBO defined**: An early developer of the MBO system describes the technique as follows: "[It is] a process whereby superior and subordinate managers of an organization jointly identify its common goals, define each individual's major area of responsibility in terms of the results expected of him, and use these measures as guides for operating the unit and assessing the contribution of each of its members."[18]

   b. **Advantages of MBO**: The MBO process requires disciplined evaluation of where an organization (or supervision program) is and where it is going—that is, it requires clearly thought out and mutually agreed-on goals, expectations, and job roles. The technique can be applied to entire agencies or to individual probation and parole supervision plans; and it has the added benefit of involving all personnel in the planning process.

6. **The Accreditation Movement**: Originally conceived by the American Correctional Association and funded by the Law Enforcement Assistance Administration, the Commission on Accreditation for Corrections was formed in 1974 to develop standards for accrediting correctional agencies. Since then, the commission has published standards for prisons, parole and probation field services, paroling authorities, jails, and other areas of adult and juvenile corrections.

   a. **Purposes served by accreditation standards**: The purpose of accreditation criteria is to provide a yardstick against which performance, facilities, and resources can be measured and to focus attention on what is needed in the correctional process. Compliance with the standards promotes protection of the general public, helps to ensure the effective administration of correction services, and works to protect the rights of offenders.

   b. **Likelihood of future development**: Since May 12, 1978, when the first four community correction agencies were accredited, numerous agencies at all levels of government have sought accreditation under the rigorous standards formulated by the commission. This would seem to assure continued movement toward accreditation of correctional agencies and personnel in the future.[19]

7. **Social and Cultural Changes**: Beyond the specific types of changes discussed above, probation and parole will be affected by broad social and cultural changes in the years ahead.

   a. **Technological changes**: Technological change has occurred at a rapid pace since probation and parole began in the late nineteenth century, and such change in the future will undoubtedly affect the corrections process. Important areas of impact are likely to be in computer technology and advanced surveillance techniques.

(1) **Computers**: The trend toward automated data-processing utilizing computers is a significant feature of modern times. Such systems now are extensively used by federal, state, and local law-enforcement agencies, and are being increasingly employed by courts and correctional agencies as well. Further automation of information processing in the future should aid correctional programs, since they require the processing and storage of so much information.

> **Impact on agency staffs**: The increasing reliance on computers for probation and parole functions will require that at least some members of agency staffs be familiar with automated processing procedures, including how to program and retrieve information on offenders. A basic knowledge of computer concepts on the part of *all* staff personnel would be helpful.

(2) **Surveillance**: Advances in technology should also permit more efficient surveillance of offenders released on probation and parole. For example, the capability currently exists to monitor the location of an offender on a continual basis with the help of electrodes that transmit signals to a central monitoring point. Such techniques could allow more inmates to be moved from prisons or jails to community-based programs; but they also have the potential to infringe on the civil rights of those released. This latter problem must be dealt with and resolved if technological surveillance procedures are to be used extensively.

b. **Increased reliance on scientific research**: To a much greater extent than in the past, rehabilitation programs and other corrections procedures are being subjected to scientific scrutiny and evaluation. This may account in part for the challenges to traditional philosophies and procedures discussed earlier in this chapter; and the hope is that such evaluation and experimentation will result in more effective structures, operations, and programs. Among other things, the trend toward increased use of scientific methods may lead to specialized research and development staff positions in corrections. Such research-oriented professionals would probably be drawn from correctional agencies (including probation and parole programs), universities, and private research organizations.

c. **Cultural changes**

(1) **Changes in values and morality**: Changes in social and cultural values can be expected as society confronts new issues and problems in the future. Perceived problems in the area of population growth, for example, have led to changing social and cultural attitudes toward birth control, abortion, homosexuality, and other facets of behavior related to reproduction and population control. Probation and parole staffs will need to be aware of trends concerning these and other social values. What may be considered "deviant" or "criminal" behavior today could be socially acceptable in the future.

(2) **Changes in laws and regulations**: Probation and parole staffs must also remember that changes in values are often the precursors of changes in laws and regulations. This calls for sensitivity and judgment by staff members in dealing with released offenders

—especially with respect to distinguishing "deviant" acts which threaten society from those which merely violate outdated laws. In exercising the discretion inherent in their role, staff members must be mindful that they themselves are part of a changing society, that they will undoubtedly react to changes, and that their subjective reactions should not interfere with fair, objective judgments in the course of their professional duties.

D. CONCLUSION

The foregoing examination of trends in probation and parole indicates that these areas are undergoing significant changes in theory, organization, administration, and services. This results from various changes in philosophy and values, not all of which may be immediately apparent. At the base, probation and parole are now in a period of experimentation in which new methods and approaches are being tried with the underlying goal of making the criminal justice system—including corrections—responsive to the needs of offenders and the public in a changing society.

NOTES

[1] David Dressler, *Practice and Theory of Probation and Parole* (New York: Columbia, 1969), pp. 73–74.

[2] Richard A. McGee, "A New Look at Sentencing," Part II, *Federal Probation*, 38: 3 (September 1974), 7.

[3] American Friends Service Committee, *Struggle for Justice: A Report on Crime and Punishment in America* (New York: Hill and Wang, 1971), p. 9.

[4] Jessica Mitford, *Kind and Usual Punishment* (New York: Knopf, 1973), p. 87.

[5] American Friends Service Committee, p. 40.

[6] National Advisory Commission on Criminal Justice Standards and Goals, *Corrections* (Washington, D.C.: U.S. Government Printing Office, 1973), p. 40.

[7] Vincent O'Leary and Kathleen J. Hanrahan, *Parole Systems in the United States: A Detailed Description of Their Structure and Procedures*, 3rd ed. (Hackensack, N.J.: National Council on Crime and Delinquency, 1977), pp. 42–47.

[8] Kenneth Culp Davis, *Discretionary Justice—A Preliminary Inquiry* (Urbana, Ill.: University of Illinois Press, 1971).

[9] Don M. Gottfredson, M. G. Neithercutt, Joan Nuffield, and Vincent O'Leary, *Four Thousand Lifetimes: A Study of Time Served and Parole Outcomes* (Davis, Calif.: National Council on Crime and Delinquency, Research Center, 1973).

[10] Maurice Sigler, "Abolish Parole?" *Federal Probation*, 39:2 (June 1975), 48.

[11] Richard McGee, "California's New Determinate Sentencing Act," *Federal Probation*, 42: 1 (March 1978), 7.

[12] American Justice Institute of Sacramento, California, under contract to the California Commission on Peace Officer Standards and Training, *The Impact of Social Trends on Crime and Criminal Justice—Project Star* (Cincinnati, Ohio: Anderson Publishing Company, 1976, and Santa Cruz, Calif.: Davis Publishing Company, 1976), pp. 26–45.

[13] National Advisory Commission on Criminal Justice Standards and Goals, p. 322.

[14] *Ibid.*, pp. 401–04; and see dissenting opinion in *Greenholtz* v. *Inmates of Nebraska Penal & Correctional Complex*, 442 U.S. 1, 1979.

[15] Paul C. Friday and David M. Peterson, "Shock Imprisonment: Comparative Analysis of Short-Term Incarceration as a Treatment Technique" Canadian Journal of Criminology and Corrections, 15:3 (1973), 287–88.

[16] Nick Gatz, "First Shock Probation; Now Shock Parole," *American Journal of Corrections*, 37 (January–February, 1975), 20.

[17] Peter F. Drucker, "Management by Objectives and Self-Control," *The Practice of Management* (New York: Harper & Row, 1954), Chapter 11.

[18] George S. Odiorne, *Management by Objectives: A System of Managerial Leadership* (New York: Pitman, 1965), pp. 55–56.

[19] "Accountability Is Emphasized as Four Agencies Are Accredited," *American Journal of Corrections*, 40: 4 (July–August 1978), 10.

A 1
B 2
C 3
D 4
E 5
F 6
G 7
H 8
I 9
J 0